In Season and Out

John Leax

Illustrated by
Roselyn Danner

ZONDERVAN PUBLISHING HOUSE · GRAND RAPIDS, MICHIGAN

Sections of this journal appeared in earlier versions in the following magazines:

The Reformed Journal

The Wesleyan Advocate

Decision

Poems appeared in:

A Time of Singing

Liberal and Fine Arts Review

Old Hickory

Cumberlands

Wellspring

For the Time Being

Judith Markham Books are published by Zondervan Publishing House, 1415 Lake Drive, S.E., Grand Rapids, Michigan 49506

IN SEASON AND OUT

© 1985 BY JOHN R. LEAX

LIBRARY OF CONGRESS CATALOGING IN PUBLICATION

Leax, John.
In season and out.
1. Leax, John. 2. Christian biography—United States. I. Title.
BR1725.L335A33 1985   209'.2 [B]   85-629
ISBN 0-310-45480-8

Designed and edited by Judith E. Markham

Printed in the United States of America

85 86 87 88 89 90 / 10 9 8 7 6 5 4 3 2 1

for my mother
and in memory of my father

In death
disturbing the ground
and memory only
as in life
to nourish it.

CONTENTS

Foreword   9

19 Torpey Street   15

Summer   27

Fall   61

Winter   95

Spring   127

ACKNOWLEDGMENTS

Because so many friends contributed their lives to the making of this book I dare not attempt an exhaustive list of their names. I ask those who appear in the text to accept their presence as acknowledgment of their importance to me. My friends who do not appear in these pages, I trust, will read nothing into their absence. The thematic structure I followed determined the incidents I narrated.

I would, however, like to name three. Professor William Greenway and Dean Frederick Shannon lightened my load so I could complete the manuscript. Dorothy Coddington transcribed my journals and typed and retyped.

FOREWORD

"I have always liked rambling, loosely organized books that can be browsed randomly. Journals are perhaps the best of these," observes the author in the entry for May 3rd. I agree. The best way to enjoy the scents, tastes, sounds, and sights of this book is to plunge right into it—anywhere. You will find every page a rich and wisely stocked cellar, sweet with the smell of earth and filled with the fruits of the year.

For those who ignore this advice (who, like me, are compulsive readers of introductions), I will try to provide an inkling of what follows.

John Leax is a poet, gardener, teacher, editor, husband, father, and woodsman who lives in the hills of western New York. His journal grows out of a deep sense of place and the faith that Christ might be apprehended in the common circumstances of life there:

> I look past the house to the trees I have planted. I look past them to the woodpile and to the garden. I hear the voices of my wife and daughter. I know all of this has come to me by grace that someday I might become a man worthy of what I have been given.

He is a man who has found his place, the right place:

> Having that one place to be—which is no place and every place—frees the Christian from having to be going anywhere but where he is.

Like Thoreau, whose journals he quotes from, Leax has "traveled much in Concord." Nothing convinces the reader more of the value of this traveling in one place than the depth and beauty of Leax's observations:

Crossing the back field, the full moon glowing above, I
felt the light as something tactile, as an element I walked
in, and I wanted to stay out, to become native to it, and
dwell in it forever.

Consider the wisdom he pulls from an old orchard past its prime:

Perhaps this is why, though I feel my failure to bring the
old orchard to fruitfulness, I feel no real guilt, why in
fact I feel a sort of pleasure in watching it turn wild and
useless. When I walk in it, it tells me that a man's caring
comes to an end. It tells me that life is lived within the
boundaries of extremes, of wildness and domestication. It
tells me that my order is not the only order. And in its
message I find comfort.

He gives us not only the beautiful, however, but also the wry, the
inexplicable, the humorous, and the homely. Here is his graphic
illustration of both our need for grace and its free abundance seen
in the antics of Poon, his hound:

I saw Poon, foul-smelling, wagging his whole hind end in
joy as I approached. A dumb beast, he understands grace.
He knows, however much his bad habits annoy, I will
not beat him for being a hound. He knows I will drag
him to the back yard, turn on the hose, and wash him.
Soaked and lathered, he will be humiliated; but cleansed,
he will be allowed in the house.

The author is a gardener whose skill one might well envy. He
has culled from the cycle of the gardener's year those entries that
pull his busy and varied life together, focus it, and let us chew on
its significance. He ruminates on everything from fishing and
gardening to the meaning of marriage and community, children,
parents, death, work, heaven, earth, writing, teaching, nuclear war,
and God. To read this book is an exercise in mental and spiritual
health; it is to receive nourishment with delight, shaken down and
running over. The author has for all of us

good gifts

....
And in my notebooks poems tilled
As jealously as the soil of this valley.

Eat, and be filled.

Robert Siegel
Whitefish Bay

19 TORPEY STREET

1

When I called Linda to tell her I had a job, she didn't say, "Oh, no!" But I'm sure I heard a gasp and an unspoken, "Back to that place in the sticks." I should have realized what I was asking of her, but I was too dense, too wrapped up in my own interests.

The desire to become a writer had governed both my undergraduate and graduate careers. Only as I began to finish my work at Johns Hopkins did I begin to consider how I was going to feed myself, my wife, and my soon-to-appear daughter. In the sixties it was easy to drift into teaching, and teaching seemed a pleasant way to survive. Since I was a Christian and had had some experience in Christian schools, teaching in a Christian college seemed logical and attractive.

Omitting Houghton, because I had graduated from there, I wrote to all the Christian colleges I could think of. None answered. So I widened my search. On my way home from an interview at a community college in the Adirondacks, I stopped in Houghton to attend the wedding of friends. Naturally I also visited with some of my professors. Before I quite realized what was happening, I was sitting across from English Division Chairman Doc Jo Rickard, a formidable woman whose classes I had avoided because I'd never learned to spell, listening to a voice that sounded like mine saying, "Yes, I'd like very much to return to Houghton."

I had grown up in rural western Pennsylvania and had spent most of my youth roaming unfenced fields and woodlots. Beyond the cornfield directly behind our house lay a strip mine so long abandoned nature had begun her slow work of healing. The sharp cuts where the bulldozers and steam shovels had dug in had yielded to gravity and erosion. Brush and scrub trees had grown up on the rounded edges, rounding them further, and marsh grasses and cattails had taken over the waterlogged bottoms. This ugly scar was one of my favorite places. But I did not love it, not the way I loved the trout streams of Clearfield County and the Allegheny River at

Tidioute and Tionesta, for it reminded me always of human avarice. Yet as my brother and I walked there, studying animal tracks and catching amphibians, I learned the rudiments of ecology in its wastes. I learned I did not like what men were willing to do to the earth, and I learned I did not want to live too close to anyone who did not value it as I did.

Linda was a city girl. She had grown up in Bellevue, a suburb bordering the western edge of Pittsburgh. Though she had enjoyed living in rural Houghton the first year of our marriage, she had regarded it as a kind of wilderness holiday, a temporary adventure without conveniences. She had given me no reason to expect she'd appreciate a lifetime there. Six weeks after the birth of our daughter, Melissa, we moved into an apartment at the edge of town and for the next five years lived snugged up against the woods. During that time subtle changes occurred in Linda. She began to learn the birds and the wildflowers, and she began to enjoy the quiet that had once driven her to distraction. When it came time for us to look for a house of our own, I suggested we look for a farm. She agreed. In principle.

Nothing we looked at was tolerable. I remember one big old house so far up in the hills I needed a compass and topographical map to find it. The real-estate broker had described it as needing "a little work." It needed to be burned down and buried. Another one, in slightly better shape, had forty junk cars behind the barn. The only one we liked had a stairway so narrow we would have had to remodel or set up our bedroom in the kitchen. It also had flies. Flies in the walls. Flies in the ceiling. Flies in the lights.

As we searched, we gradually realized we were fooling ourselves. We could not have moved to a farm, if one had been available. A few years after we were married, Linda had had a stroke. As a result, for the second time in her life she had to learn to talk and walk. For months I had stood by helplessly, watching her struggle, admiring her courage. Only after those immediate obstacles had been conquered did we begin to learn the pernicious ways the stroke had changed our lives. Every funny pain, every headache sent us into panic. In those moments we relied on the closeness and understanding of our Christian friends and neighbors. We needed them often, and we needed them close.

When we first saw the house for sale on Torpey Street in nearby Fillmore, we thought it handsome. We also thought it expensive. The large, white, Victorian structure rose, a formal mass, from luxuriant, dark green arborvitae and dominated its neighbors. It wasn't us. Still, whenever we drove past it, we wondered. Finally one snowy day in January, almost whimsically, I stopped.

I stepped into a large living room. Directly ahead of me white pillars framed the entrance to the dining room. To my left French doors opened into a paneled den. I liked it. I thought, "Linda will love it."

That afternoon the two of us returned. Though I had no idea what I was doing, I squeezed into the crawl space off the dirt basement to shove my knife into the sills, and I climbed into the attic to examine the ridge pole. I'd heard those were the things to do when you looked at old houses.

We moved to Fillmore in April. Though we were excited about owning our first house, we did not expect to stay long. A few years, long enough for Linda to grow stronger, and we would move on; if not to another school, at least to another house. Two things changed that.

When Doc Jo asked me to return to Houghton, she may have known what she was getting me into. I didn't. I knew that I was returning to a community that had welcomed me and encouraged me when I wasn't sure how much welcome and encouragement I deserved. I knew also that I was returning to a countryside to which I felt a deep personal attachment. It was the countryside where as a young man I first began to feel happiness. And it was the countryside to which I brought my wife and where we had lived the first year of our marriage. What I hadn't foreseen was that in my own house, absorbed in the responsibility of caring for it and the small plot of earth surrounding it, living among people I loved, I would begin to learn the meaning of being at home.

My writing and teaching reinforced what was happening in my inner life. I began to understand that writing is a means of taking thought, a means of affirming what I want to be. My abstract desire to make my writing a part of my servanthood gradually became concrete. By writing I learned that what is written is the least important end of the writing process. I learned that what mattered was the work taking place in me. By teaching the writers whose work I value most—Henry David Thoreau, William Carlos Williams, Thomas Merton, Wendell Berry—I found reasons to stay. Studying their lives, I learned the aimless nomadism so characteristic of American literary careers is unnecessary. Berry, for example, abandoned New York City and returned to his native Kentucky. Home, he discovered himself "growing out of the earth like the other native animals and plants." Williams, another writer who stayed in place, said much the same thing when in his old age he suggested that the only reason to write poems is to become a better man. Thoreau cautioned against the nineteenth century's version of the space shuttle, calling it an "improved means to an unimproved end." Recognizing, like Berry and Williams after him, that there is no better place, that the improved end, a better man, must find its beginning in discipline enacted in the place where one is, Thoreau did most of his traveling in Concord.

This discipline of placedness is presented in Christian terms in the work of Thomas Merton. In his life and in his writing Merton affirmed that the Christian has only one place to be. In Christ. Having that one place to be—which is no place and every place— frees the Christian from having to be going anywhere but where he is. As I understand this, by choosing to stay where I am, where Christ has placed me, I act out in my life my resting in Him.

None of this is easy. But when I drive up to the house at 19

Torpey Street, I feel a sort of joy. I look at the massive white front rising nearly three stories above me. I look past the house to the trees I have planted. I look past them to the woodpile and to the garden. I hear the voices of my wife and daughter. I know all of this has come to me by grace that someday I might become a man worthy of what I have been given.

Some days, as I enter the house, I hear rising from deep in my memory the exchange between Warren and Mary in Robert Frost's *The Death of the Hired Man.* Warren speaks first: "Home is the place where, when you have to go there / They have to take you in." And Mary replies, "I should have called it / Something you somehow haven't to deserve."

2

This journal about staying in one place began with a journey. In the fall of 1977, after nine years of teaching, I took a sabbatical leave. We packed a small U-Haul trailer with a bunch of books, a season's worth of clothes, kitchen utensils, and dishes and moved to Wilmore, Kentucky, for four months. During those months I audited course work at Asbury Theological Seminary and traveled two days a week to Louisville to work at the Thomas Merton Studies Center. Though I put many miles on my car, I worked leisurely, spending much time with Linda and Melissa, and catching up on books outside of my academic discipline. Paradoxically, the time I spent in Kentucky confirmed the commitment I was making to stay in western New York.

In October, partly because my scholarship required it, partly because my spirit desired it, I made a retreat at Our Lady of Gethsemani, Merton's monastery in Trappist, Kentucky. As is the custom, I made my retreat privately, without a director. The silence of the Trappist life frightened me, for it was more than an absence of sound; it was a positive presence. It was the silence of the voice that speaks all things in himself. I fled from it. I went out of my room, walked the hills, and took photographs of the monastery.

The second afternoon on retreat I began to feel comfortable, and I began to reflect on what the hours I was spending would mean to me when I left. One thing was clear. In the monastery the whole schedule was arranged to remind me I live in Christ. In the silence I had faced my calling to making images, to seeing through them the Christ who is the creator of all images, to living out the implications of the incarnation in my daily life. Outside the monastery, I would have to find a way to keep these truths present in my consciousness.

Without realizing it, I already had a habit that would help me do that. All my writing life I had worked with a set of images that bear witness to the presence of Christ in the world. In Wendell Berry's essay "Discipline and Hope," which I reread shortly after my stay at Gethsemani, I found them systemized.

According to Berry, a system of interlinking analogies lives in our speech and in our experience. He calls them an "expansive metaphor of farming and marriage and worship." This metaphor or set of relationships comprehends all human experience. "A farmer's relation to his land," Berry argues, "is the basic and central connection in the relation of humanity to the creation; the agricultural relation stands for the larger relation. Similarly, marriage is the basic and central community tie; it begins and stands for the relation we have to family and to the larger circles of human association. And these relationships to the creation and to the human community are in turn basic to, and may stand for, our relationship to God—or to the sustaining mysteries and powers of the creation."

Once I recognized how these relationships were charged with spiritual import, I had my way of keeping the presence of Christ in the world and my life in Him in my consciousness. Everything I look at I also look through to Him.

When I began the journal that makes up this book, I set out to observe the workings of these relationships in my life. Consequently what is recorded here is personal. It happened to me. But it is not merely personal. Because we all live within the same context of relationships, what I experience can be made clear to you. Whether you live in the city or the country, I have written in the hope that these observations will help clarify the presence of Christ in your life as well as mine.

*. . . be instant in season,
out of season . . .*
2 Timothy 4:2

SUMMER

His name is Al. He's an old bachelor, and he makes the neighborhood his business. If there's anything I want to know, he's the man to see. But he mumbles. And he never refers to a house by its current owner; he identifies it by its builder who died before I was born. Consequently, a conversation with him can be a trying experience. Still, I can't imagine a more considerate and conscientious neighbor; I look at the care he lavishes on his house and yard, and I give thanks.

Sometimes, however, his conscientiousness is a source of tension. His only work is his house and yard. My work includes teaching, writing, family, woodcutting, gardening, and more. Often things must go undone around my house and yard. When they do, he notices.

The other day, for example, he stood in front of my garage and muttered, "You got everything in there but money." He's wrong. A good portion of my money is tied up in the collected junk I store. Some day I'm going to have a garage sale. But for now I can't let anything go. Something might prove useful.

This morning over coffee I heard another of his remarks. He told one of my friends, Willis Beardsley, who is the college registrar, "You know, if Jack worked half as hard at a real job as he does on his woodpile and garden, he could afford to heat with gas and buy canned vegetables."

June 23

Though I am only three days into summer, I am more than a month into my summer break, and I feel as if time is getting away from me. I have no reason to feel this. My garden is on schedule, I'm getting in the wood, and all is well. Perhaps I just find it hard to be patient, to do one thing at a time and allow a job to come to completion at its own pace. It will happen that way whether I fret or not. My single responsibility is the work before me.

Today's work was splitting wood. As I sit here writing, my fingers are stiff from the grasping of ax and sledge, and I find it difficult to control the fine motions necessary in writing. Thoreau insisted that a scholar who labored in the woods or fields would write truer sentences for his effort. I suspect he would have been more accurate had he said "fewer sentences." Tonight as I came across the yard around 10:30 after walking the dog, the heavy sweetness of the split oak lay in the air like a dark bass line under the treble lightness of the mock orange.

June 28

It's been years since I sat in the classroom on the student's side of the desk. This morning I changed that and enrolled in a seminar on poetry writing with William Heyen SUNY College at Brockport. I was excited for I admire Heyen's poetry, and I wanted to see how he goes about teaching.

June 29

A week or so ago, rereading Heyen's first book, getting ready for the class, I was stopped short by his poem, "Birds and Roses Are Birds and Roses."

> I have come to rely
> on the timeless in the temporal,
> on the always faithful inner-eye,
> on detail that deepens to fond symbol.
>
> But all morning the sun found
> feathers scattered under a bush
> where roses had fallen to the ground.
> The remains of a thrush.
>
> I would flesh this one bird's feathers,
> resume its quick eye and lilting trill.
> But these were not the mystics' flowers:

their bush cast a shadow like a bell.

The poem shook me, for the first stanza accurately describes a process I have come to rely on in writing my own poems—fact giving rise to metaphor and symbol. Working that way, I have often been pleased by the convergence of eternity and time. But almost as often I have been shocked by the fact that refuses to open into enlightenment. Poems confronting those facts are born in darkness; they are ghastly truths clothed in beautiful words.

The first session of the seminar was curious. I enjoyed Heyen's quiet refusal to say more about poetry than can be said, his refusal to tell someone else how to write a poem, and his refusal to allow someone to tell him how to write a poem. Having long ago come to the conviction that my words must be my words, and that I must stand by them, I was amused by the protestations of the students who wanted to be taught. In my own classes I always find those students the most difficult to work with. They seem to have no sense of the distinction between being taught and learning. When the class ended, I knew I was going to enjoy the seminar.

But throughout the two hours I had been bothered by a nagging cough. Since the afternoon activities were informal, I decided to come home and rest. By the time I was halfway home I was feeling dizzy and wishing I had someone with me to take over the driving. By the time I was home I knew I had a fever, so I went to see Dr. Prinsell. He stuck his stethoscope on my chest and pronounced, "Pneumonia. Bed rest for a week."

July 1

Through the window beside my bed I can see Linda working around the apple and cherry trees we planted this spring. She has a small spray bottle and is dealing death to the aphids clustered near the tips of the branches. As I lay here, I am remembering the storeroom at Kelly Brothers where we bought those trees. The air was heavy with a damp, loamy smell that actually felt good to breathe. Sucking it in I could almost imagine myself a tree drawing the richness of the earth into my roots and stretching my top to the light.

The afternoon we bought our trees it rained, so we had to wait a couple days to plant them. When I started to dig, I expected to find heavy, wet soil, but spring had been so dry that only the top inch or two, those inches held together by grass roots, contained moisture. I set each tree, filled the hole halfway with soil, and then ran it full of water.

While I waited for the water to soak in, I pruned. That was hard, for I tend to put my faith in the seen, not the unseen, and the budding tops looked strong. But I followed directions. Since the roots had been reduced by one-third to one-half in transplanting, I nipped the branches off the same, bringing the size of the tree into conformity with its source of nourishment.

Brutal as it seemed then, I can see in the lush green of their present flourishing that it was good.

I would like to work the same good on a small orchard planted years ago by a forgotten farmer in a meadow near the middle of the woodlot we own with Brian and Margaret Sayers and Rich and Beaver Perkins. Each February or March I think of getting out the saws, but late winter is a busy time on campus, so each year ends up the same:

> Too late
> to hike the old roadbed
> to the little meadow
> where a generation ago
> someone set out an orchard.

> Too late
> to prune the twisted trees
> for while we huddled,
> zealots in the night
> of winter's rule,

wild spring worked
a silent coup.

Too late
to think of apple flesh
crisp and white.

Too late
except anarchic grace yield
a crop apart
from works of mine
to think even of cider
from the culls
fallen in the grass.

Those trees, arranged so haphazardly on a knoll fast being overrun by brush and thorn apple, loomed large in my consciousness as I drove through the carefully groomed orchards of central Ontario in June. I marveled at the neatness of the Ontario orchards, but I also felt vaguely oppressed by the unnatural sameness of the ordered rows. Reflecting on my double response, I am beginning to understand what troubled me.

A small orchard gracing a hillside, pruned to bear, is a sign of a man's caring. It fits into a scheme of many hills and many orchards, a scheme of many men caring. But an endless orchard, thousands and thousands of trees, fits into no scheme except the scheme of the market and the desire for profit.

Perhaps this is why, though I feel my failure to bring the old orchard to fruitfulness, I feel no real guilt, why in fact I feel a sort of pleasure in watching it turn wild and useless. When I walk in it, it tells me that a man's caring comes to an end. It tells me that life is lived within the boundaries of extremes, of wildness and domestication. It tells me that my order is not the only order. And in its message I find comfort.

For two days Linda and Melissa have been picking and freezing strawberries and peas. Both are so sweet it is as if they've been sugared. The raw peas are almost as—no, in their own way they are every bit as delectable as the strawberries. Melissa must think so too, for this year she is enjoying the work.

I'm finding my enforced inactivity frustrating; it's hard on my self-image to watch Linda and Melissa do everything while I sit and read *Moby Dick*. Yesterday Dr. Prinsell told me my lungs are clearing, but he also told me I have another ten days on antibiotics and two more weeks of limited activity.

Since he didn't define limited activity, I'm defining it for myself by trial and error. This morning I helped Melissa get her rabbits ready for the Bible-school small-animal zoo. We hauled the hutch from the garage, cleaned the nesting boxes, and burned the old hair and dung from the wire with a torch. How I've come to be tending rabbits is a story with a moral.

Our friends Larry and Bonnie Christensen and their three daughters, Kim, Kara, and Kathie, live in a three-family intentional community called Celebration Farm. One day last fall Melissa announced that Kara was giving her a pair of rabbits for Christmas. I doubted it, since neither Linda nor I had heard anything about it from Bonnie or Larry, but I went along with the discussion for fun.

"What would you do with a rabbit?"

"Eat it," Melissa answered.

"No!" Linda was firm.

"Why not?" I goaded.

"Listen," she said. "I ate your catfish stew. Nothing you say is going to make me eat fried bunny."

The rabbits we were talking about hadn't been born yet, so we dropped the subject. Yet like the heady odor of hoya blossoms, it remained in the atmosphere of the house. When the November

Organic Gardening arrived, I couldn't resist reading out loud from an article, "Animals Fit for the Garden."

> Rabbits require even less space than chickens. Every three months, one male (buck) and one female (doe) can provide your family with 16 pounds of all-white meat, fine grained and tender. They would need only 12 square feet of cage space.

"You couldn't kill a baby rabbit to save your life," Linda answered.

"They wouldn't be babies," I said. "They'd be fryers."

"Big difference."

For the next few weeks we discussed exchange and the sacramental nature of the food chain. We agreed that everything we eat was once living. We agreed that saying grace over a meal includes being thankful for the shed life represented by the meal. We agreed that every time we eat we recall the Lord's Supper. And we agreed that while we acknowledge these things in theory, we prefer in practice to keep the death involved as far from us as possible.

That is what led us to get the rabbits. Just once, we decided, we should bring the death close.

The moment they wiggled their little black noses and nuzzled their first carrots from our hands, however, they became bunnies, permanent residents displacing the family car in the heart of the garage. Determined, I invoked plan B. Our bunnies would be breeding stock; we'd raise a litter of fryers. In late February we bred them. The weather began to break, and I had occasional afternoons to work in the yard, clearing up, getting ready to put in peas. Metaphors of Easter and new life began to inhabit the garage.

Then one Sunday afternoon, Melissa called me to come see Poppa Rabbit. He was sitting hunched up and refused to move. His right hind leg was broken, snapped cleanly in half. I called

Larry and asked to borrow his .22. He said to bring Poppa to the farm where we could dispose of him away from Linda and Melissa.

Whether for ourselves or for Poppa, we moved very gently toward the death. I lifted Poppa from the box I'd carried him in, cradled him in my arm, and showed Larry the break. "That's the awful part of having animals," he said. "Things go wrong." He loaded the rifle, and I placed Poppa on the ground facing away from us. The .22 spat, and a blood rose appeared on the back of Poppa's head.

At that point, we hoped at least to salvage a meal. But when we skinned him we discovered that he had somehow also broken his foreleg, and that the extensive bleeding from the injuries had spoiled the meat.

A few weeks later, when she was due, Momma failed to kindle, and we faced our failure. The ritual enactment of exchange we planned had gone completely awry, and we had nothing to show for it except a small black pelt nailed to the garage wall.

We replaced Poppa with Charlie, a neighbor's no-longer-wanted pet, giving us another pair. But we don't expect to breed them. We expect only to feed them and carry nitrogen rich pellets to the compost pile.

The exchange we sought will have to wait until fall when the spring lamb we've bought is ready for slaughter.

July 4

While my fellow Americans were celebrating, I was bathing a dog. Poon, my half-breed, all-useless bluetick hound did his usual and found a pile of manure to roll in. I did my usual muttering, dumped a bottle of honey-and-wheatgerm shampoo over him, and commenced scrubbing. My only consolation as I got wetter and wetter was that he hadn't been skunked.

Nothing cleans a skunked dog, or person for that matter.

Whatever it is that carries that lovely odor is absorbed by the hair, so not even tomato juice, the stand-by folk remedy, can cut it.

A curious thing happens to humans who tangle with skunks. Their nose hairs absorb the odor, so they sneak around trying to keep their distance from their friends because they think they stink. And indeed, to themselves, they do.

An analogy comes to mind. The same thing occurs when we sin. Long after the noticeable consequences have passed from our lives, long after those around us have ceased to be offended by our reek, we live in the stench of our actions, for they have become a part of us. And like skunk, it takes more than tomato juice to restore us to an acceptable state.

July 6

We sat out on the deck until 11:30 last night before we decided not to wait up until the eclipse. At 2:30 I hauled myself out of bed for a look. A small quarter moon remained, and I could see the progress of the earth's shadow across it. So I stood and watched until nothing remained but a faint red glow from the lower right-hand section. The corona, which I had gotten up to see, wasn't visible.

This morning, when the dog got me up at six, the sun was rising gorgeous rose.

July 7

Though we've hardly used it since we wheelbarrowed wood to the truck last summer, the path into the woods is still clear. The planks we flopped across the ditch, however, are gone, making my entry a jump from clearing to thicket. For the first hundred yards the path weaves through soft maple, fire cherry, and thorn apple that we have left uncleared as a barrier between our work and the road. At the edge of our first work area, an acre or two of soft maple we thinned and planted with black walnuts a year ago, the path loses itself in the openness of the forest floor.

I've come for two reasons—to see if the walnuts are growing and to see if the red raspberries spreading in the light we made are ripe. I can find no signs of the walnuts, but the berries are glowing purple and soft. They are not at their height yet, but enough are ripe to justify coming back with Linda and Melissa.

Since I am alone and do not have a chain saw with me, I am almost silent as I move across the opening. The woods are alive with squirrels. Wherever I turn I see leaping gray or red shadows. A small red squirrel poses motionlessly on a stickup. Several more scold me from the protection of the bushes beneath him. Suddenly they burst like a covey of birds and explode up tree trunks in every direction.

On the far side of the work area the path again becomes distinct, threading between the monstrous wolf tree and the grove of wrist-thick, soft maple saplings it has seeded over the years. Someday we will have a lot of work to do in this grove, but this morning my mind is not on work. I am watching the tracks in the soft earth of the path and hoping to see a deer.

The path turns and runs up a knoll through some large red oaks and peters out on the needled floor of the only pine grove in our woods. It is a good place to sit, and I have seen deer in the brush at its edges. So I sit. I can hear warblers, but the heavy foliage they prefer keeps them hidden.

Walking again, I follow the path down off the knoll toward the abandoned railroad, but I bend away from it and cross the stream to a second knoll. This knoll has been logged, and we have spent many weekends cutting tops and hauling cordwood to the trails and then home. To look at it this morning though, you would hardly guess how often we've invaded the quiet with our saws and tractor. The canopy of young oak and maple spreads into a roof. Sunlight still gets through, but there is no sense of the devastation so frequently left by loggers.

Instead of climbing the knoll and going on—the land stretches nearly a mile further—I go a little ways along the stream to the foot of a particular oak I've kept marked in my head for eight months. Last November I discovered a dead dog under it and wrote a poem:

> The big, mixed breed hound grins
> from his rest under the oak.
> His eye is glazed.
> His belly is collapsed
> beneath his ribs.
> His carcass is frozen
> to the ground
> and dusted with snow.
>
> The acorns falling on his hide
> did not kill him,
> but they will sprout
> from the corruption of his death.
> Curled under the tree, this beast,
> the friend of man
> now friend of worms
> shapes a question on the earth.
>
> What delectable evil did he taste
> in the last foul mess he sniffed
> to leave him leering so
> at every walker in the wood?

This spring when we hauled out the wood we cut last fall, the fact of his death was so much more pungent than it was last fall in the snow that I did not write about it. What was left of his flesh had melted into a shapelessness almost unrecognizable as dog. Today there is no odor, and the shapelessness is increased.

The fleshless bones have been scattered into a position impossible in life. The metaphysical question of my poem has vanished from my consciousness. All I want to know is how the skull moved from the head of the spine to the cavity of the rib cage.

The question, of course, is unanswerable. So I retrace my steps and start back up the path to return to the car. Before I go far I see a deer trail winding off the path, and since we have been considering making a looping path for casual walking, I decide to follow it. It takes me along the crest of the bank above the railroad and then down onto a mushy flat below the wolf tree. Just as I decide I am in an area of the woods I have never been in, I see the stumps of some ironwoods we cut for posts, and I step into the light of our first work area.

Ahead of me I see more raspberries, and at my feet tiny, wild strawberries. I pick a handful and head for the car.

July 10

My activity is still supposed to be limited, but I cheated today and did some fairly heavy work in the garden. Melissa picked the last peas yesterday, pulled the vines, and piled them on the compost. Knowing that double cropping in western New York is tight (frost can come early), I went next door, lugged Bruce's Rototiller out of his basement, did up the plot, laid out the rows, and called Melissa to help put in the beans. That was cruel of me, for of all the vegetables we grow she likes beans the least. In truth she hates them. But I let her do the yellow beans, which she tolerates, and we got on well.

When the beans were in, we mulched the potatoes, planted a third crop of lettuce and radishes, and put in the fall turnips. Then we moved the rabbit hutch out of the garage and set it under the mock orange for the summer.

Though I feel good about getting the work done, and better finding I'm well enough to do it, I'm suffering from a mild case of the guilts. The Houghton Wesleyan Church is divided into what we call shepherding groups. Each group is made up of five to ten families, which are charged with helping each other. Our group, all families from outside of the town of Houghton, meets once a month for a meal and fellowship. Often we combine that meeting with a work bee. Today the group helped the McWilliamses move. All the while I was working in the garden, my friends were hauling furniture thinking I was too sick to help.

Around 4:30 I showered, dressed in neat clean clothes, went to the after-work picnic with the group, and ate as if I'd been working.

July 11

We lived about a mile down the road from Louie Kuznik when I was growing up. I got to know him because he rented the field behind our house to grow feed corn for his pigs. One year I helped him with the harvest. He drove his tractor and wagon into the field, parked, and gave me a small ring with a sharp, hooked blade protruding from it. I put the ring on my middle finger so that the blade stuck out from the back of my hand. I pulled the corn, shucked it, trimmed it with the knife, and then tossed it onto the wagon.

I did that all day. And I didn't get paid. A boy playing at a man's work, I wasn't fast enough for wages. Instead I was invited up to his orchard to pick a few bushels of apples for my mother. Picking apples turned out to be worse than picking corn, for Louie let his pigs run in the orchard, and he had a mean old sow that outweighed me by 500 pounds. She chased me up a tree and kept me there until Louie came out to see why I wasn't finished.

What brings this back is Robert Siegel's book of poems *In a Pig's Eye,* which I've been rereading. The first poem, "Ego," compares the human ego to a raunchy pig rooting and rutting in the garbage of the world. The image pressing itself on my mind is of a divided self—the ego pig at the base of the tree keeping the better self clinging in fear to a swaying branch. Though it has been more than twenty-five years since I hung there, I still sense a part of me up some tree waiting for a Louie Kuznik to come out of his barn, play Christ to my need, and set me free of my devouring self.

July 12

Today I'm thirty-nine.

Thirty-nine wasted years.

Just a minute, Buster, I haven't wasted . . .

Buster yourself. What do you know now that you didn't know at twenty?

Well . . .

Do you know any better who you are?

That's an adolescent question.

That's a complacent answer. Do you?

Well . . .

You're stalling for time, and at thirty-nine you better believe it's running out.

I'm a child of God.

That's a theological platitude taught twelve-year-olds.

Stick it in your ear; I have work to do.

What kind of work?

My father's.

The old image of Christ bit huh?

Yes. What of it?

Nothing.

Nothing?

Precisely. Without definition it means nothing.

Ah! There I've got you. My work is words. I define things.

Connotation or denotation?

Connotation. The meanings keep changing.

At least you're honest.

For the moment.

Most people register surprise when I tell them I have taught at Houghton for fourteen years. Academics move. That is the way to promotion and prestige. I have nothing against either, but I intend to stay put, for in an age of nomads I want to be a placed person. Curiously though, I am not placed. I am native to nothing around me. I stay by volition, recognizing that I am misplaced, hoping that by staying misplaced long enough I will at least come to rest.

Last night, while walking Poon, I suddenly realized I had walked past nine houses within one quarter mile of mine and did not know the occupants of any of them. I can rationalize my ignorance. The generation gap accounts for part of it; most of the houses are occupied by elderly couples or widows who keep to themselves. The cultural gap figures in it too; college English profs are not easily assimilated into the daily life of a small rural town. And the inevitable knowledge gap between old and new residents finishes it off; I've only been in this town nine years—I'll never possess the local knowledge of those who go back generations.

It is my fate to be alien. The few acres I am native to in western Pennsylvania are gone, buried under shopping malls and housing developments. But like a weed swept from the hold of a ship, I am determined to find a niche, to dig my roots into the soil of this place I have come to.

Sometimes, in another mood, I am able to see the nature of placedness from a different perspective, one that is more positive and comforting. I have been describing the local pole of placedness. There is a universal pole also, the earth itself. Wendell Berry points out that they are the same. The doorstep is all of the earth that one can comprehend in any given moment. The rest is abstraction.

Putting this into explicitly Christian terms, I can say I have been placed by the will of God on this earth for specific purposes (which I must discover) for a specific length of time (which will always be unknown to me). As long as I maintain the awareness of these terms of my living on earth, I transcend any local alienation I feel. Any place I stand is home, for my home is earth.

July 15

A small job is one nobody notices unless it is undone.

July 16

Morning is prelude.

The cardinal shrills his call
from the tallest poplar:
We two we two mine mine mine.

And the hound, baying
like he means business, runs
his daily rabbit to its hole,
then slinks back panting.

Blackberries for your cereal
glisten in the tangles
along the road.

The day's work begins.

July 19

A little over a week has passed since I put in the beans. From where I sit on the deck I can see them, and they are a good four inches tall. This hot, humid weather complete with afternoon thundershowers is ideal for them. No infestation of bugs or onslaught of slugs can keep up with their growth. It would hardly be an exaggeration to say I can see them growing. But I can't.

What I can see, not moment by moment, but season by season, is the growth of the soil in the small beds where I raise root crops. From the compost and mulch I've spread over the years I've been gardening, the beds have risen three inches higher than the lawn around them. Over those years I've grown fond of compost. I crumbled some "finished stuff" in my hand the other day and wondered that the wastes of my life can be so profitably conserved. But so much is in perspective. Last night I came across a poem in Whitman that contrasts and balances my response. He wrote:

> Now I am terrified at the earth, it is that calm
> and patient,
> It grows such sweet things out of such corruptions
> It turns harmless and stainless on its axis, with
> such endless successions of diseas'd corpses.

Seeing through Whitman's eyes, expanding my vision through his, I realize that there is something terrifyingly "other," something alien to the human in the fecundity of nature, in the ability of the earth to absorb offal and make itself. It is terrifying to realize that humus is not inert. It is, according to John H. Storer, a "hive of living things. . . . The bacteria alone may range from comparatively few up to three or four billion in a single gram of dry soil."

I suppose in looking at compost I am looking at a sign of the resurrection, of life proceeding out of death. But I have a hard time accepting the analogy, for it is badly flawed. In nature the life that rises out of the dead is never new life for the dead; it is always merely another life feeding on the one that died. The resurrection begins a life unimaginable within the confines of nature.

July 23

Tonight is a spectacular night for stars. There are so many I am confused by their abundance and cannot sort out any constellation other than the Big Dipper. When I walked up behind the mill to get out of the streetlights, the Milky Way came clear and reminded me of what a cloud would look like on a photograph negative—a wash of white. After standing in the mill's shadow for several minutes, I saw one of the points of light was moving. Clearly it wasn't a plane. I thought maybe I was seeing a satellite. Then suddenly it halted its apparent horizontal movement, plunged earthward, and went out.

Before going into the dark to watch the stars, I had walked along the edge of the grass between the road and the backwater from the river. Quiet ruled. No frogs croaked as they did last night and the night before. I thought about the system my brother and I used for poaching frogs for froglegs when we were teenagers. I handled the bow rigged with a reel, squidding line, and a fishing arrow. He handled the light. When a frog croaked, he held it in the light, and I shot down the beam.

I rarely missed, but it made me uncomfortable. Like so many of the lower creatures, frogs seemed to have no vitals. No matter how I shot them, I reeled them in spitted, but leaping, and had to smash them against a log or stone to kill them. I have no doubt I could still shoot a frog, if I knew it was going to be eaten, but I could not do it so cruelly. Nor could I do it against the law, out of season and at night.

August 1

Early last spring Larry Christensen gave me a couple hundred cuttings of hybrid poplars, which grow to firewood size in five years. I planned to plant them in the woodlot meadow and harvest them for free firewood as part of the church's wood-for-fuel project. But it didn't work out. I wasn't able to line up the help I needed to clear the meadow, which is growing up in thorn apple. I got them out of the refrigerator this afternoon and found that apart from a little mold they are still in good shape. I called Larry to see if he wanted them back, and then took them up to the farm. He and Bonnie will put them in a seedbed and try transplanting them next spring.

I had envisioned the quick-growing poplars as one pole of my stewardship. The other pole was to be the infinitely slow-growing walnuts we planted last fall. That neither is in place and growing leaves me with a sense of double failure.

I will try both again. But I have lost a year.

*　　*　　*

All day Saturday as we worked in the woods, I watched the tractor wear and compact the path. Our tractor is light, and we are careful, but by afternoon the earth was marked by our presence. It will heal in a few seasons, for the path we made is crooked, twisting around saplings and trees that will grow into timber. As they grow, they will drop their leaves and build the soil beneath them, gradually erasing all traces of our labor.

Climbing on and off the tractor, I began to recognize that my angle of vision and my ability to relate to the nonhuman altered as I changed my position. On the tractor I saw trees and concentrated on steering around them. I was a power, apart from the woods. Walking, I saw woodpeckers and red efts; I moved more as a creature that belonged. But riding or walking, I was aware of my separateness from the rest of nature.

Some writers on ecology and some poets would have me comprehend this separateness as alienation. It seems to me that a better term would be distinctiveness. I am not a pantheist. I do not want to be taken up in the sameness of the All. I want red efts to be red efts. I want to enjoy the individuality of each part of creation, experiencing it as something other than myself. Admitting this distinctiveness does not diminish my ability to be related to the nonhuman. Rather it defines the terms of the relationship. It admits consciousness into my living and allows me to stand apart from the world without denying I remain a creature of the world.

We've been in Pittsburgh for a week. Mother had planned a birthday picnic and reunion for Grandma at Adam's Falls. It didn't come off. A few days before her birthday Grandma fell coming out of the house at Aunt Ginny's and broke her hip. A friend of ours, a doctor's daughter, told us that that is inaccurate. Her father says elderly people fall because their hips give out and break. However it happened, her hip is broken, and what reunion we held, we held at her bedside. She had quite a time coming out of anesthesia, but by the time we arrived, she was pretty much herself. The first thing she said to me was, "Whoever thought you'd see your grandmother stuck in a hospital bed."

*   *   *

One afternoon while we were there, I walked up and down street after street in Bellevue, where we lived the semester I taught at Robert Morris College and where Linda's parents still live. As I walked I tried to imagine what it would be like to live there again. At first I felt the obvious impossibility of living the way I choose to live within the confines of an old suburban neighborhood.

Where would I garden?

How could I avoid total dependence on power companies?

How could I tolerate the nitpicking regulations—park here Wednesday, park there Thursday, have garbage wrapped and on the curb Friday?

Then I began to think rather than react. Most of the outward manifestations of my lifestyle would change, but my lifestyle itself, because it is not a surface affectation, would not. The disciplines I embrace because they are right disciplines would remain. The greatest benefit of my gardening, for example, is not the economic value of what I grow. It is not even the high quality of my produce. It is my involvement in the process of caring, of growth and renewal. It is my awareness of my place in nature. That awareness I could maintain, if I worked at it, with a window box or a small border of flowers.

The only advantage of country living over city living is the visibility of the relationship. Here in the country a failure in the garden is seen in terms of a shriveled plant. In the city it is seen in terms of higher prices. Ultimately, in city or country, the terms are the same.

August 8

When I walked Poon last night the darkness seemed greater than usual. Stars were out, but haze diminished them so their light seemed far away and powerless. I felt vaguely restless, at loose ends, and spiritually cold. Sometimes the immanence of God in the things of this world is hard to perceive. His transcendence seems so great I despair of ever knowing him. He seems wholly other, as apart from me as I am apart from the dog I was walking. He seems apart in the same way too—not uncaring, simply beyond.

A quarter mile down the road I realized I'd walked further into darkness than I usually go. Then over Snyder Hill, just above the woodlot, I saw a thin slice of orange. Poon and I stood still and watched the moon rise until it broke free of earth and floated in the sky.

I can't say my spirits rose with the moon. But I learned a long time ago to trust God's character and not my momentary feelings about his presence.

August 10

Linda and I took the canoe up to Silver Lake tonight. We didn't bother fishing. We just puttered along the north shore enjoying whatever we happened to see.

Islands, as small as fishing boats,
anchor in the bay.
A dozen gabbling ducks,
dunking and splashing, ignore
the flames leaping across the cirrus sky.
Afire we drift
through a field of water lilies.
In the shallows a grounded willow
rises and falls as the wind
swells the evening lake.

In its branches a green heron
waits for a yellow perch
or speckled frog
to flash within his reach.
Complete in himself,
he knows we threaten nothing
he can eat,
and our quiet paddles,
at their most violent,
cannot rock the floating world
he stands in.

August 12

Tomorrow is payday, and I'm preparing for a jolt. After banking four checks, which were swollen to twice their normal size by the government money I earned administering the faculty development section of the college's Title III grant, I'm about to return to normal. Facing that, I've been doing a little accounting. The roughly $2000 extra I've had left my hands in the following ways:

None of the money was wasted, but I am embarrassed that the largest sum went to paying off things I am already wearing out. And I have more to pay on them. This failure of stewardship troubles me not only for itself but for its weakening of my argument that stewardship involves more than money. If I can't manage the simplest of the stewardship disciplines, what right have I to urge others to consider the more complex ones?

draperies, bathroom floor and sink	$ 400
doctor bills and drugs	150
car repairs	200
vet bills	50
payment of land loan	125
payments on accumulated debts	650
chimney repair	65
given away	300
Total	$1940

My comfort is the sense that though the consequences of past sins remain in my life, the sins themselves have been forgiven. Guilt need not interfere with my getting on with correcting what needs correcting and with establishing more appropriate habits. This means conserving what I have now or doing without until the balance I allowed to be lost is restored. And frankly, I find that hard. Everything in the culture around me urges instant gratification.

August 13

Yesterday Poon refused to go out for his morning run. I didn't think much of it at the time; he skips it occasionally and then barks to go out midmorning. But as the day passed, he lay in a patch of sunshine and did not move. His eyes clouded and he whimpered. By four o'clock he could barely get up, and he was tender to the touch. I called the vet.

This morning I could not talk him up to get him to the car. Neither could I roll him onto a blanket to lift him; he howled at the slightest pressure. One of my friends, Roy Bielewicz, raises

Great Danes, so I called him. Together we got Poon onto the blanket and into the car.

The vet found general but no localized pain, no swellings or injuries. He said Poon, who is only about six, is exhibiting symptoms of a very old dog—possible prostate trouble or spinal arthritis. He gave him a shot, put him on painkiller and an antibiotic. I'm to watch him.

August 15

Mother is visiting. This afternoon we went hiking along Wiscoy Creek where we collected a batch of wildflowers, which we have spread over the dining room table. Mother has the field guide open, and every few minutes she or Linda calls out an identification.

"It is Joe Pye Weed! My memory was wrong."

"This has to be Purple Showy Milkweed."

"Jewel Weed."

"Purple Flowering Raspberry."

"No. That doesn't look right."

"Sure. Look at the star pattern of the finished blossom."

"Yes. I guess you're right."

Though I'm interested in the flowers and determined to learn not only their names, but at what time of year and where they blossom, today I was more interested in watching the fish. I'd never been on the Wiscoy without a fishing rod. Being there without one so changed my way of relating to the stream and the fish that I found the large suckers working the middle of the pools as fascinating and beautiful as the brown trout lurking under the overhanging ledges and tree roots.

*   *   *

Poon is responding to the antibiotic, which means he doesn't have arthritis. When we came in with the flowers, he followed me up the stairs for the first time in four days. He still shows weakness in the hindquarters, and his gait is awkward, but he's acting more like himself.

August 27

Though I worked on it all summer, when faculty retreat ended at noon yesterday, I hardly noticed. One of the writing faculty members resigned to write a novel, and we're frantically adjusting schedules and rearranging classes.

August 29

Frost the last two nights. Gardens up on the hills are gone, and the cornfields up and down the valley have suffered severe damage. We were lucky. I misted the garden around midnight both evenings to give it some protection, and it worked. A few leaves on the bean plants are black, but the blossoms are holding. Probably the greatest danger to us is the sustained cold that is slowing their growth and will, if it continues, make getting them in before the September frosts unlikely.

The low temperatures led to the discovery that the blower motor on my furnace is out. I cleaned the chimney and fired up the wood stove—the earliest I've ever burned.

* * *

Our community service wood-for-fuel project—a simple matter of dropping a few trees, cutting them up, splitting them for stove wood, and then giving it away—has caught the eye of some Washington bureaucrat who has written it up as a press release.

51

What irony that this life-long Democrat has become an example of Reaganomics at work!

September 1

A few mornings ago when I was filling up at Bill Yanda's Quaker State, Bill got to talking about the end of the world. He pointed out the station door to the park across the road and shook his head. "Look at that beautiful world," he said. "To think that it's fallen! You just can't imagine it made new!" Another customer pulled in, ending our conversation. But as I drove off, I was surprised at how intensely I felt what Bill was saying, for I've never been much interested in talk of heaven. I've never felt it was necessary.

After thinking about it the last few days, I'm convinced that heaven's unnecessariness is what makes it important. It's important because it has no relevance to this life. (It does not follow that this life has no relevance to it.) Heaven is simply a glorious, gratuitous extra, totally unnecessary, but totally in character with the extravagant goodness and boundless creativeness of the Maker and Redeemer of this world.

September 2

Heavy rain today toppled the overgrown lilacs and dumped them onto the garden. They broke several leaves off the Brussels sprouts, but did no serious damage. The weather, however, remains troublesome; the cold and wet has brought growth to a halt. The hope of beans declines daily. If they get frosted, or just plain fail, it will be the harshest blow to our garden ever.

September 4

Thin ground fog tonight. Crossing the back field, the full moon glowing above, I felt the light as something tactile, as an

52

element I walked in, and I wanted to stay out, to become native to it, and to dwell in it forever.

But I came in, out of the experience into reflection upon it, and began this writing.

Though it is Saturday and still summer, I spent the day at autumn work. The morning I gave to a training session with the student tutors who help with freshmen writing. The afternoon I gave to the woodpile, first putting a new handle on the ax and then splitting. I've done sixteen facecords since June. Another truckload or two and I'll have two years' supply on hand, finally, after four years of burning, getting into a proper cycle of cutting, aging, and burning.

The wood split, I went up to Larry's where we shot and dressed three ducks. Our actions took on a symbolic weight, for we had to shoot them behind the barn rather than in the yard where we cleaned them; Kara's rabbit kindled last night and we couldn't risk upsetting her or the four babies in the hutch with her. Charlie is the poppa. When I got home, I had Melissa give him a carrot in lieu of a cigar.

September 6

The sudden caffeine overload from the office coffeepot, along with the normal excitement of the new semester, has made it difficult for me to get to sleep the last few nights. And the dog across the street has taken to barking, making it even more difficult to stay there. Around one last night I gave up, took a book out to the kitchen, and finished the raspberry yogurt as I read. A deliciously cool breeze, too cool for the peppers and beans, drifted through the window and chilled my arms almost, but not quite, to the point of discomfort.

There! That paragraph illustrates what I tried to tell my fiction class today. I started out headed for a thought and ended up with goosebumps. The writer's world is the world of sensation, not the world of idea. His task, my task, is to show how one points to the other.

September 11

I wasted my time worrying about the beans. Yesterday was in the 90s. Today is in the 80s. Bent over in the sun, I sweated through both my shirts, baked the soreness from splitting wood out of my back, and picked a half bushel of green beans. An equal number of yellow beans awaits my attention tomorrow.

September 12

Mike Walters, our new pastor, preached his first sermon this morning. If he quit tonight, I would remain thankful for his ministry, for almost as an aside to the main point of his message, he gave me a new way to look at petitionary prayer, a subject that has troubled me for years. He said simply, "God is not displeased when we remind him of his promises; it shows we believe he will fulfill them."

* * *

Two weeks of trout season are left. Now that the beans are in, I'm hoping for cold nights to bring the browns up from the holes and start them feeding. Lloyd Wilt, a colleague in the English department and longtime fishing partner, and I went out last night. He took one; I lost another. But the chubs drove us crazy. Tap. Tap. Tap. I must have caught fifteen of them before the trout hit and so surprised me I didn't set the hook.

* * *

Last summer I erected a board fence across part of our lot near the back of the yard. Behind it, out of sight, I have my chopping block and woodpile. Close by, underneath the mock orange, I have the rabbit hutch. Friday I was splitting wood and came to a stubborn piece, so I grabbed the chain saw, revved it, and set it to the wood. I forgot how close my work area is to the rabbits, and I forgot how skitterish they are, how easily they panic at sudden movements or noises.

Momma Rabbit went berserk. She charged around her pen shaking the hutch so violently I heard her over the saw. I shut it down and, speaking softly, moved to calm her. But before I could, she barreled into the side of the pen, bounced backward, and lay, eyes glazed, twitching and snuffling. All I could see was Poppa Rabbit and the .22 rose on his head.

I opened the cage and examined her. Finding no broken legs, I raised her into a sitting position, caressed her, and talked as soothingly as I knew how. She responded; the fear slipped from her, and in about fifteen minutes she was quietly crunching a carrot, pulled fresh from the garden and offered in repentance.

For three days I've been thinking about this incident; I keep returning to what must be a cliché—the easiness of death, the quickness and permanence of it. When we shot the ducks last week, we shot the first one under the eye instead of over the eye. The duck, of course, was dead but didn't know it. Hanging upside down from my hands, dripping blood onto the ground, it tried to raise itself. In that moment I knew regret and sorrow. But the deed was done. Nothing could withdraw the gentle pressure of the finger on the trigger. Nothing could restore liveliness to the limpness swinging against my leg as I rounded the barn to the yard and the bucket of scalding water.

Minutes later, plucked and gutted, ready for the table, the duck was not even recognizable as having been a living thing.

This morning as I headed for work, three eighteen-wheelers and twelve tractors pulling hoppers were lined up along the commercial beanfield near Houghton. By lunchtime the tractors were crawling over the field like huge clanging insects, spewing beans into the hoppers behind them. One eighteen-wheeler was loaded. A second was half loaded, a worker standing on top of the beans raking them higher. When I came home tonight, only three tractors remained. The field was picked clean, but the air was pungent with bean.

September 16

A dream: I came out of my office in Fancher Hall into bright sunshine. Suddenly, though I remained in the same place, I was in darkness. Those around me, students and friends, were still in light. I floated up from the steps out over the lawn and settled on my back under one of the young birch trees planted last spring. My friends followed me. Their voices sounded worried; I could hear them saying things like, "We have to help him, he's having a breakdown."

I wanted to tell them that they were disturbing me, that I was perfectly happy there in the grass looking up at the stars, but they kept touching me, tugging at my arms, begging me to get up. I think they called an ambulance. But I was adamant and floated away. I think I was pleased watching them grow smaller and smaller. Then the stars went out.

September 20

Nearing the equinox. The end of summer. A starless night with rain as soft as spring, a rain that smells of spring as it pebbles the dust in the library parking lot. There will be no frost tonight.

But in the house it's cold. The furnace is still out, and we've been too busy to tend the fire. Instead we've piled on sweaters and ignored the chill. Linda is studying for her class. Melissa is asleep. I'm grading papers so I can return them before leaving for Long Island where I'll be doing some poetry readings.

The yearly adjustment, our transition from the laconic rhythms of summer to the staccato duties of academia is nearly complete. To my pleasure, I'm finding I can already call up the faces of many of my students as I mark their work.

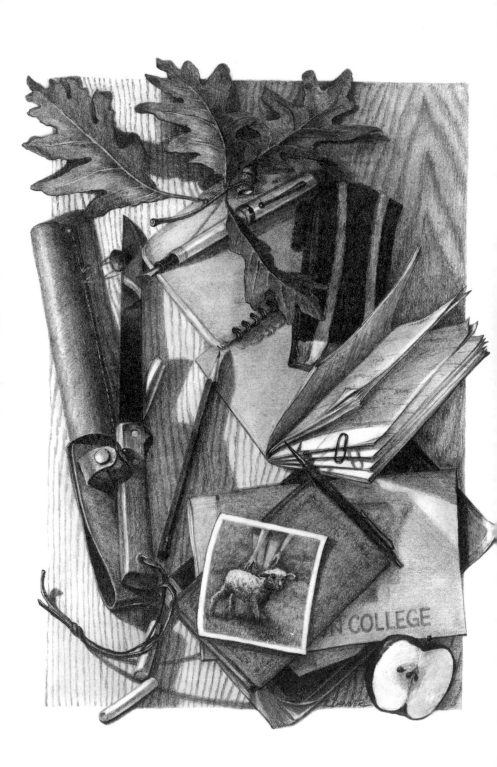

FALL

The equinox passed unnoticed while we were on Long Island, and now night has the upper hand. Soon Orion will appear in the east and begin his long stalk across the sky. As the cold comes on, we will gather near the stove, abandoning the distant rooms, working in the pleasant distractions of each other's presence, waiting out the winter.

*   *   *

When we arrived home last night, we found a note from Sandy Bielewicz:

> Roy has been feeding the cat, but she hasn't eaten since you left. Saturday he looked for her and found her under the table in pretty sad shape—not able to get up and breathing in gasps. She wouldn't eat. He came home to get me. She meowed a few times but didn't seem responsive. I picked her up; she felt limp. I wasn't sure what to do, so I gave the vet a call. He said, at her age there wasn't much he could do. She worked her way back under the table even though she couldn't get up on her back legs. I left her and will see what happens. Hope you don't come home to bad news.
>
> Sandy

In Roy's handwriting the note continued:

> I found her dead behind the stove. Sorrowfully, Roy.

And then his father's writing:

> Jack—I put her in a box in the garage. I'm awfully sorry.

The cat, variously called Cat, Kitty, or Beast, was nearly seventeen years old, three years older than Melissa. I had gotten her for Linda a few weeks after we were married; she was one of the givens of our life, a weekly expense, a loved annoyance. Linda and

Melissa cried. I held them, and then with Melissa went out to the garage.

I raised the cover from the box. Kitty's eyes were open. A flea, obscene as death itself, crawled from one of them. I put the cover down, picked up the shovel, and went out into the rain.

Standing in the middle of the yard, I considered where to dig. Under the mock orange? The pussy willow, Melissa's favorite tree? The larch. I dug under the tree I brought from Pennsylvania as a memorial when, after my father died, we sold the home he'd built. When I finished, Melissa lined the bottom with newspaper. I lifted the cat from the box, held her a moment, then laid her on the papers. We covered her and filled the hole.

Without our knowing it, Linda had watched from the window.

Last winter, realizing how the cat had shrunk from her thirteen-pound prime to less than half that weight, I wrote:

> The old cat whose calm
> dwells among us
> has taken up residence
> by the stove.
> Her gums are spotted.
> She weighs no more
> than her dreams.
>
> She is a seed
> of golden fur secured
> to the world
> by claws honed
> on the velvet chair.
>
> Soon a wind will lift
> her from the warmth,
> and we will find
> her gone
> into the sleep she dreams.

The geese, honking and squawking, began their flyover today. When we heard them at supper, we ran out to watch, but we didn't grin foolishly at each other as we do in the spring. We stood quietly and felt a chill.

* * *

Last night I lost my temper with Melissa, who was up after midnight doing her algebra. I wasn't really angry with her; I was tired, impatient, and generally fussed at my inability to keep from overextending myself and trying to do too much. She merely got between me and my annoyance. After I apologized and she went to bed, I told Linda, "For two cents I'd scrap this book, sell the land, sell the house, move into an apartment, lounge in Izod pajamas, and live out my life reading murder mysteries."

Tonight, though nothing in the world has changed, I have a better hold on my emotions. They are dangerous things. If they were all I had to go on, I'd give up this difficult stewardship I've accepted. Fortunately, commitments are made with the intelligence and stand against the onslaught of feeling.

After my reading at St. Joseph's on Long Island last week, I was asked why I don't write about anguish and the threat of nuclear disaster. I answered, "I do. Anguish and disaster is the context we live in.

> Rumors of war
> disturb my sleep
> and fears
> of the end
> of all life gnaw
> my joy.

We all know that. I want to say, by my life and by my words, that it is possible for it to be otherwise. To do that, I accept responsibility for the things I can touch. I commit myself to the work of bringing wholeness to them."

Last night my emotions told me that task is too big for me. Probably they are right. Against the destruction of the earth, I can offer only my weakness. My hope is Christ, who has chosen to make weakness his strength.

* * *

I realize, of course, that responsible lifestyles radically different from mine are possible. I've made the choices I have because I'm blessed with physical strength, because I enjoy labor, and because I live where I am free to so choose. Other men make other choices and make them in the will of God.

I choose to own my home, to burn wood, and to garden because I want to live in visible relation to the earth. I want others to see what responsibility I have accepted, to know why I have accepted it, and to hold me accountable for my actions. I want it because this is an age that evades responsibility and accountability.

Some of my friends, however, refuse to own homes because this is also an age in which men have forgotten that there is no such thing as ownership. They choose to rent, to care for another's property to demonstrate the principle of stewardship. Their life discipline is as valid as mine.

September 30

Poon and I have just come in from looking for Orion. If my star chart is right, he is there, but the moon is full and outshines the stars. I know there is nothing magical about the moon; that pock-faced old man staring down at me is a geologic formation. Yet I always feel a wonder in moonlight, a drunkenness that has nothing to do with the tingling in my nostrils from the fermenting grain at the feed mill.

Standing quietly in the yard, I could hear leaves falling.

Melissa has raked a large pile of them. Saturday we'll spread them between the Brussels sprouts. They're almost ready, but they need a good hard frost to freeze their bitterness away.

I borrowed Bob Brown's decrepit pickup this morning, backed it up to the garage, and started loading. Before I was finished I'd loaded six bags of garbage, five months worth of newspapers, one worn-out rug and assorted pieces of rug padding, a burned out charcoal grill, one tire from my '69 Falcon (which I sold in '75), a broken zim-zam game, a broken bowling game, two ruined toasters, a rubber doormat, scraps of chicken wire, several outdated textbooks, a shattered tennis racket, the first fishing rod I ever owned, a stack of rusted pots and pans (last used on a camping trip in '75), silverware to go with the pots, my best slippers and work hat, a hamster wheel, a toad cage, a box of styrofoam packing, the rusted screen from the screen door I fixed last spring, and two neighbor boys, Matt and Scott Reitnour, who wanted to visit the dump. I threw out everything but Matt and Scott and felt considerably better for it.

Tonight with the car in the garage I feel so proud I may even invite Al neighbor over for a look. But I'm too tired; my responsibilities on campus, which are heavier than usual, keep me one step behind, tense, and sometimes hard to live with. Still, I find it rewarding and, except for a little more control of the pace, would have it no other way.

For the past two weeks I've been watching a student struggle with an essay about the slow, painful death of her grandfather. The subject weighed on her a little heavier than she expected, and she was tempted to give it up. But crying as she wrote and choking back tears in my office as she talked about it, she persisted and finished. She doesn't yet know what she has accomplished. She doesn't know that she has passed from being a student to being a writer. And she doesn't know, probably will never know, how I rejoice in her success, how I find encouragement and hope in work such as hers.

October 3

We have cut flowers on the table. The rose bush is loaded with buds and the tomatoes are thriving!

*   *   *

This morning at communion the sun reflecting from the passing trays played across the ceiling and turned the sacrament into a dance of light.

*   *   *

This afternoon as I was sowing rye for a cover crop on the garden, Melissa told me she was glad we live the way we do. When I asked her what she meant, she said, "You know, growing our own vegetables organically and freezing them together. And burning wood. All the things we do to try to live right."

I'm glad she's glad. And I'm glad she told me. I need some assurance that at least one of the inheritors of earth shares my values.

> The Patriarch of Fear believes
> in platitudes and in the power
> of bombs to make them true.
> At his word the earth could die.
>
> In the echo of his rhetoric
> I pick late beans,
> pull the spent plants for compost,
> and begin turning the ground
> to receive a green manure.

66

The soil is rich with worms;
the lure of autumn bass—one last
night on the river—tempts me.
But the Fall's discipline
is to return to students,
to move across the garden
sowing the restoration
of the earth.

October 5

I arranged to meet my students this evening, while Linda was at choir rehearsal, instead of this afternoon, so I could work in the woods. Rich and Brian had gone out ahead of me; when I reached the turnoff onto the old railroad bed, I could hear their saws. But I decided to park and walk in the path. It would only take a few minutes longer than driving, and I wanted to see how the woods had changed since I last walked them in July.

Though the yellow-gold layer of poplar leaves that covered the path was occasionally splashed with maple red, most of the red remained brilliant against the sky, and the green had not even begun to drain from the stubborn oaks. Still, as I walked, I walked in the rainfall hiss of dropping leaves.

A hundred yards in, where we cleared the thorn apple and thinned the maples, the raspberry canes obliterated the trail. Parting the canes, paying more attention to their prickers than to where I was going, I strayed east of where I meant to be and wandered into the grove of young maples before I even realized I'd left the path. My good intentions about cutting a nature trail through the area came to mind, and I thought about how difficult it's going to be to keep it open. I still want to make one, though, for I made so much noise in the brush that I neither saw nor heard bird, squirrel, or chipmunk. The only sounds persistently loud enough to rise above my dry slogging were the chain-saw snarl and tractor chug in the distance.

The waiting work moved me quickly through the pines and down the hill to where Rich and Brian were pulling tops from the creekbed. I grabbed my saw from the trailer and set about firewooding a tangle of tops on the slope, working slowly, thinking only about keeping my feet planted under me and my saw under control. Though I've been cutting for several years now, I'm still not at ease with the saw. It's too big, too fast, and too loud. Neither am I completely at ease with the little 1937 Allis Chalmers tractor we use. When it suddenly slips sideways, jouncing through one of the corduroyed gullies, panic flies up my throat. Deep in my mind, below the level of casual talk, I know that no matter how long I work in the woods, I am a bookish man, that my labor to be safe must always be conscious. Brian's caution, "There are more ways to buy it in the woods than you can imagine," is a warning I do not take lightly.

Last year a red pine twisted as it fell and willfully chased me around the woods. Fortunately it could only see yellow, and when I knocked my hard hat off on a low branch, it was content to fall on that.

After cutting for an hour or so, I shut the saw down to rest. As I placed it on the ground, I saw, brown-edged and soft, what was left of a carpet of May apples laying on the humus they were becoming. I looked around carefully and realized I was working in my favorite part of the woods, the part I gravitate to in the spring when the Jack-in-the-Pulpits blossom. Today in the autumn, the dry streambed flooded by leaf fall, it is a different world.

October 7

I'm approaching forty. Today, for no reason I can discern, I've had a feeling I'm no longer the man known by my friends, that every conversation I begin is an effort to reestablish a common ground. Suddenly I'm afraid that I have to remake all my friends and that time is running out.

The risk involved seems so great I wonder if I can fake it.

Thursday I went to hear a poet I've much admired. I heard a broken old man who fumbled with his book, spilled his water, worked his lips chewing the air, drooled, and, finally forcing words from his mouth, spoke in a thin unsteady voice that could not make the sounds of his poems. Though listening to him was agony, I felt a bit of wonder, for I attributed his mannerisms to a stroke and saw a triumph in his standing before us.

As he read from his newest book, I heard the voice of affirmation, the voice of the religious faith he'd rejected fifteen years ago, returning. And I thought, "Illness can do that for a man." And then I thought of Elliott Coleman, the wonderful, virtually unknown poet I studied with at Johns Hopkins. I visited him once in his old age. Broken by a stroke, the elegant Anglophile I knew had become a bearded, wild old man, a Whitman on the streets of Baltimore. At lunch he rose on his cane and declaimed, loud enough for the whole restaurant to hear, "I never wanted to be old; I never thought I'd be old; and now that I'm old, I don't like it."

Later in the afternoon, in a quieter moment, he remembered serving communion in a military hospital during World War II. Tears filled his eyes and made a grim contrast to his gesture of dismissal, "But that was my Anglican period. I don't believe anything now. The first thing to go, you know, was a belief in the afterlife. Once that was gone," he shrugged, "nothing." I quoted one of his new poems and tried to talk of the dark night of the soul. He wouldn't hear of it. "If you want to think of it that way," he said, "okay. But it's not. It's nothing. And when the time comes, I know where the pills are."

He didn't use the pills. But he died confessing nothing.

What started this brooding on illness and loss is a celebration.

Today is Houghton's centennial homecoming. One of my former students, who is studying at the university where the poet I heard Thursday teaches, told me the man has never had a stroke. He is suffering the last stages of chronic alcoholism. The only thing driving him back to his faith is guilt and fear.

And grace.

But what drove Elliott Coleman in his last days? If God is faithful to complete the work he begins, why did he allow Elliott to die in darkness and despair?

October 10

Parrot green,
the summer snake curled
on the fall warm bed
of the railroad.

"Kill it!"
cried Matt and Scott
grabbing for stones.
I stayed their arms.

"You like snakes?"
Scott asked.
"We need them,"
I answered.
"This kind eats
spiders, snails, and slugs."

"Huh!" scoffed Matt.
"Howcum, if they're so good,
Satan's one?"

October 12

It may be Indian Summer during the day, but tonight it's blowing cold. The wind wails, "Winter, winter, winter." When I took Nanna Greenway home a little while ago, she leaned on my arm going up her walk and said, "You haven't got a decent choice, Jack. Either you get old and wobbly, or you die."

October 14

Since making the drive to Long Island a couple weeks ago, I've been having muscle spasms in my back. Tonight I'm all tightened up, so I settled myself in the recliner by the fire, turned up the heating pad, and read the book I bought in New York, *Peace March,* Millen Brand's poetic journal of the annual Nagasaki to Hiroshima trek. It is a simple, moving book. As I read, I looked across the room at Melissa who was born on August 6, the anniversary of the bombing of Hiroshima. In my imagination I hold her life against the futility of nuclear war. Over the summer she read *The Hiroshima Diary* and John Hershey's *Hiroshima*. Her response still rings true, "Why would we do such a thing?" A couple nights ago Phyllis Schlafley ticked off the "peaceniks" in her column, quoted Scripture to justify the arms race, and self-righteously claimed the world was safe as long as we were the only ones with nuclear arms. Her argument is beyond my comprehension. Two A-bombs have been dropped in war. Both were dropped on civilian populations. We, the people of the United States of America, dropped both.

Even if one grants, which I won't, that the destruction of Hiroshima can be justified, how does one explain away the gratuitousness of the destruction of Nagasaki? Why would we do such a thing?

The question is important for the unthinkable is happening. In Ronald Reagan we have a president who calls peace activists communist dupes, who manipulates language, labeling the MX "Peacemaker," and who imagines a protracted, winnable nuclear war.

71

"The bomb exploded within 100 feet of the aiming point. The fireball was 18,000 feet across. The temperature at the center of the fireball was 100,000,000 degrees. The people who were near the center became nothing. The whole city was blown to bits and the ruins all caught fire instantly everywhere, burning briskly. 70,000 people were killed right away or died within a few hours. Those who did not die at once suffered great pain. Few of them were soldiers." (Thomas Merton, *Original Child Bomb*)

Nothing, absolutely nothing I value can be preserved by the power of nuclear weapons.

October 15

I have two friends. With one I share my aspirations. With the other I share my doubts. With neither am I whole. I swing from doubt to affirmation, always exaggerating my true position.

Once I had a friend with whom I could share both and find a balance. My life is too rich for me to say I'm lonely, but I know his absence deeply and miss the hours we laughed the outrageous world into perspective.

October 18

A friend was going to help, but he forgot; so Larry and I were left to do it ourselves. We put some grain in a small feeding trough beside the barn door and let the lamb out of the stall. Since it had had nothing but water for twenty-four hours, it went straight for the trough, lowered its head, and began eating. Larry shot it between the eyes. A swift trickle of blood streamed from the forehead, and the lamb, after an instant in which it seemed to pause registering surprise and betrayal, leapt four feet into the air tucking its forelegs to itself as gracefully as a deer clearing a fence, came down running, covered the twenty feet between the barn and pasture gate, stopped, and turned. Larry shot it again, and it dropped without a sound.

We grabbed it by the legs, heaved it into a cradle we had placed over a clean bed of hay, and awkwardly, accidentally grabbing the bloodied wool of its head to stretch the neck taut, I slit the throat. The wool resisted the knife; I had to part it with my left hand and slash with my right. When I hit the spinal nerves, the legs thrashed. I thought of my mother asking me if I'd "murdered that poor little lamb yet" when she called yesterday. But I felt almost no emotion. The need to work quickly and gently allowed no time for sentiment.

As soon as the lamb bled, I cut through the neckbone with a meatsaw and removed the head. Both Larry and I felt better.

The warm afternoon turned cold and dusk came on as we went about what proved to be hard physical work. I had hauled twenty cords of wood before starting the lamb, and by the time we had it hanging to remove the fleece, the pain in my bum shoulder had my upper arm screaming for mercy. We switched on the light and kept working, fisting the hide from the carcass, our hands alternately freezing in the air and warming inside the lamb.

Accustomed to thinking analogically, I kept expecting the metaphorical import of our work to weigh on me. For weeks, as I anticipated the slaughter, the lamb had existed in two worlds. But fact refused to yield its primacy; even when I reached into the chest cavity, pulled out the heart, and dropped it into salt water to soak, the literal lamb dangled by the tendons of its hind legs before me.

Only what was happening to my hands startled me. Buried in the body of the lamb, they changed. Woods hard, scraped, and battered, they grew soft as they worked against the fat under its skin, and when I washed them in a bucket of water and scrubbed them together, I felt a strange womanly smoothness I did not recognize. I held them to my nose and breathed the tallowy sweetness of the lamb's death.

Work to do before the snow comes to stay:
1. rebuild storm window for living room
2. repair and hang back storm door
3. clean porch for stacking wood
4. stack six cords of wood dumped on lawn
5. harvest broccoli
6. harvest Brussels sprouts
7. pull carrots
8. spread compost
9. cut peonies, snowballs, and ferns and compost
10. cut and mulch roses
11. haul manure from Larry's
12. dress garden
13. cover garden with hay mulch
14. bring tractor down from woods
15. sell the house and move to the city

October 30

Matt and Scott's four-year-old brother, Brian, has been in and out of the hospital for the last two weeks. He has viral pneumonia, which has caused rashlike lesions to erupt all over his body. The nurses have told Kathy, his mother, that he wanders from his room to the playroom muttering, "It takes too long to get well. It takes too long to get well." For the most part, however, he has accepted his hospitalization fairly well. When we left him tonight, he was helping one of the nurses empty the wastebaskets and practicing a question for his doctor, "How's my epidermis today, Doc?"

The real strain has been on Kathy. A single parent, she not only has to meet Brian's special needs, but also the needs of Matt, Scott, and Lori, who feel her haste and preoccupation with Brian's illness. Apart from these family pressures, she also has to keep up with a full academic load at the college.

We've done what we could to help, a meal now and then, a ride to the hospital. In all the chaos of the disruption a small moment of tranquility has isolated itself in my memory. One evening after dinner Scott wanted me to sharpen his pocketknife for him. I got out my stone, oiled it, and showed him how to do it himself. He was quickly bored and asked, "Why can't you do this for me?"

"Are you old enough for a knife?" I answered.

"Sure," he retorted.

"Then you're old enough to take care of it yourself."

He went back to work. The image of him bent over the stone in the circle of brightness from the dining room light is an image of hope, an image that can stand against the pain and worry of these days.

November 1

For the last two weekends I've been working on the community service wood-for-fuel project. Easy work this year; the woods were dry, the day was warm, the tractor was running well, and we had our new trailer. Last year was a different story.

The ground hadn't frozen yet, but two inches of wet snow had fallen. As we walked, hauling logs on our shoulders, we tramped mud paths and soaked our boots. Our gloves soaked even faster, and we froze. About ten o'clock Roy Chandler arrived with the tractor we had just bought from him, but it didn't help. We had no way to get across the ditch between the railroad bed and the woods. So we slogged and sweated bearing poplar crosses. At the end of the day I drove the tractor the mile down the hill and parked it in the backyard.

Here I have two confessions to make. First: our tractor is so old, so conveniently small and unsophisticated, so slow on the highway, that the local farmers in their big enclosed Fords actually laugh when they roar past me on the road. Second: in spite of their laughter, coming through town the first time, my old leather jacket flapping, my watch cap pulled over my ears, the four cylinders chugging and popping, I felt downright rural.

Linda told me that my mother, who had watched my arrival from the window, had shaken her head and exclaimed, "I don't believe it. For this he prepped at Stony Brook."

November 3

The pain in my back has been getting steadily worse. Last week I started to lose feeling in my right arm, so I went to the doctor. He suspected arthritis in my neck and sent me for X-rays and physical therapy. I spent this morning at the hospital, coming away with good news. I don't have arthritis; I simply have a messed-up back. The therapist located a knot the size of a golf ball in my right shoulder. When she pressed it, my body jumped as if I'd been shocked. She found a second knot in my left shoulder, told me my neck was taut enough to play like a banjo, and that the rest of my back was swollen and inflamed.

During the nearly six weeks I've been this way, expecting the trouble to correct itself if I ignored it, I've hauled over forty cords of wood. What a jerk! This afternoon I couldn't believe how good I felt; I'd forgotten what it was like to stand up straight.

*   *   *

Brian is home. He must be kept quiet for two months or his lesions might recur. And as a side effect from the pneumonia, he has arthritis.

Anyone want to ponder the nature of suffering?
"Not I," said the duck.
"Then I will do it myself," said the little red hen.

> The chicken house came down
> when Pap started dying.

One summer night Butch pitched
a tent on the level spot
where it had stood and announced
we were sleeping out.

He was eleven. I was six.
I can't remember who got scared first.

But the sharp distinction
between the natural dark
and the mellow, human light
in the house
fell like dew on our sleep.

We fled together
and huddled in the light
of Pap's mocking grin.

The dark, however, ruled the day.

Pap died.

November 4

A dream: Linda and I are at Letchworth Park or somewhere in the Adirondacks. We are hiking an easy trail. Many people are around. No one seems to notice, but the trail runs along a precipice. Far below I see a small river.

I am afraid for Linda and try to stay close to her, but she is leaping and laughing along the edge without care. We come to a small gully that cuts through the path. To go on we have to descend into it and climb up the other side. "It's dangerous," I say. "Let's go back." Linda starts down the bank. I can see loose stones, but she makes it easily.

The moment I divert my eyes, watching my feet as I follow, she is sliding out of control. I reach out to grab her. She is inches from my hand. Without uttering a sound, she plunges over the edge.

A long wail escapes me. I hear it. I know I am making it, but it is as if I dwell in my scream. I watch her fall, her limp body bouncing and sliding all the way to the river. On its bank she lays still. I know she is dead. I dwell in my scream.

Then, suddenly, she moves, stands up, and waves gaily. I run down the face of the cliff as if it were a meadow.

November 5

Lovely light this afternoon. Around four I was driving northeast. Heavy snow clouds loomed ahead of me, but behind me in the southwest the sun, low on the horizon, shone from a brilliant, blue sky. A beam of gold shot under the clouds lighting them from below. It looked as if the corn stubble fields were alight, sending up the stored sunshine of summer to hold off the winter dark.

* * *

The few moments before bed, when I go outside to walk the dog, feed the rabbits, and split kindling for the morning fire, are often the most peaceful of the day. I love the comfort of the soft garage light glowing against the dark, the rustling of the rabbits in the hutch, the smell of the hay, and the feel of the old hatchet that belonged to my father. Tonight is one of those good nights. The clear sky promises dropping temperatures, and for the first time this season I see Orion hanging low on the eastern horizon. I almost shouted when I saw him, faithful, old winter friend!

* * *

Unfortunately many things have been omitted which should have been recorded in our journal, for though we made it a rule to set down all our experiences therein, yet such a resolution is very hard to keep, for the important

78

experience rarely allows us to remember such obligations, and so indifferent things get recorded, while that is frequently neglected. It is not easy to write in a journal what interests us at any time, because to write it is not what interests us. (Henry David Thoreau, *A Week on the Concord and Merrimac Rivers*)

November 8

Linda and Melissa have gone to a party and left me at home with Poon. To be helpful, I decided to freeze the Brussels sprouts so they won't have to do it tomorrow. What a job! It's worse than snapping beans. Beans are forthright vegetables; if they're bug-eaten, they show it, and I can chuck them without a second look. But these sprouts are like some people I've met—nice and clean on the outside, rotten on the inside. I had to get to know each sprout personally before I could judge.

As I worked, I thought about the nature of my commitment to this place where I live, not just to my job and the people I work with, but to the place itself, this house on an eighth acre of river bottom smack in the middle of Fillmore. A small house on two or three acres of land that I looked at ten years ago may be coming up for sale. The possibilities of that place still live in my imagination. I can see the house, the neat, clean barn I'd build, the garden, the hillside orchard I'd plant, the writing shack at the edge of the woods. The desire for "something better" is always with me. But I've learned that undisciplined, that desire is a distraction. It does nothing but lure me from the task at hand. Disciplined, indulged as a fancy, as I indulged it working tonight, it serves as a measure. It helps me see how I'm doing with my river bottom.

November 9
Current Issues Day

Once a semester the student senate selects a topic for discussion and invites a group of speakers to address the campus community. This semester's topic is Issues in Managing Our Wilderness.

Between speakers I developed a rather elaborate statement leading to a question I didn't ask:

Most preservationists extol the virtues of the nonhuman world and emphasize the importance of realizing human insignificance in the presence of creation. Christianity sees man as set apart, subject to the Creator, but not even in his presence insignificant. The Genesis mandate to subdue and have dominion over the earth, according to Loren Wilkerson in *Earthkeeping,* is so strong it implies rape and plunder. The mandate, of course, must be understood in terms of the continuing revelation of all of Scripture. The many servanthood passages in the Old Testament soften the violence of the mandate, but they do not contradict it. One cannot think about "The Lord is my shepherd" too long without remembering that a shepherd shears his sheep and finally consumes the mutton. However generous his caring may be, it is not selfless. (Melissa took a lamb sandwich to school yesterday and recited to her friends:

> Once I had a little lamb,
> My father shot it dead.
> Now it comes to school with me
> Between two slabs of bread.)

The point of the shepherd's caring seems to be the preservation of a principal adequate to guarantee interest to live on. In other words, the servanthood is as much self-oriented as other-oriented. The observations on the way all species alter their environments for their own purposes, which René Dubos records in *The Wooing of Earth,* suggest that a species can survive no other way.

The question I didn't ask: Isn't a strictly preservationist view the result of grafting the anti-human strains of oriental philosophy onto a healthy rejection of arrogant humanism, and isn't this grafting incompatible with a Christian view of man? If the answer is yes, might we not argue that what sets man apart from the animals is his awareness of the consequences of his actions? That awareness, in turn, might be the factor that makes man responsible. Could we then argue from and successfully demonstrate the ecological necessity of the higher serving the lower for the preservation of both?

November 14

A month ago I made a list of fifteen jobs to do before snow. We have an inch this morning, and I'm nine tasks short of finishing. Still, an afternoon and one good Saturday should be enough to catch up.

Besides this journal, I've been working on a long poem I've been commissioned to write and then read at graduation next spring. For awhile I thought I knew what I was trying to say, but I've got more started than I can easily resolve. Coming up with as little as I have has left me depressed so that I wonder if my struggle to find the word is worth the effort. Will I know any more of reality when I'm finished? Or will I only know a batch of words that came out of my head?

One of the things I'm learning as I sit at this typewriter day after day is that my writing isn't as important to me as I thought. It isn't unimportant; I expect to keep at it until they haul me away. But given any particular occasion where I must choose between my writing and some direct human involvement, I will choose the involvement. I haven't come to this conclusion without a struggle. Dorothy Sayers' argument that her writing was her involvement has held much appeal for me, but more and more I think of myself in terms of Wordsworth's characterization of the poet as "a man speaking to men."

In his introduction to my chapbook *Shoring the Ruins,* Lionel Basney called my poems "utterances, something the poet would say, something the poet did say." I like that. When I'm writing, I like to think I'm talking over the fence to my neighbor or drinking a cup of coffee with a bunch of friends. That kind of talk is crucial to community, but it's dropped when someone needs help. Helping, working with each other, takes precedence. Sometimes, when the community is healthy, when the work is going well, the talk goes on as we labor. Then the talk is really good. My writing is the same; it's best when I've yielded it up to get at the real work. Then it just happens. Like talk. Like a jest at my own expense.

November 18

An afternoon spent hauling manure and dressing the garden was clarifying. Few tasks are as fundamental; fork after fork onto the truck up at Larry's, and then fork after fork off the truck in the backyard. The very nature of the work—the hands and the back (which held up pretty well) occupied, the mind free to wander into the future, into the growth of next year—is affirmative. It begins in dullness and ends in faith.

After doing the garden, I went around catching up on all but one of those jobs to do before snow. As I worked, I thought about my small chores in relation to the larger labors that engage Larry at the farm. Though the scale of my work is smaller than his, the discipline we accept is the same—the stewardship of the parcel of earth we've been given. There is in fact no other discipline. That so few recognize it, and that fewer accept it, simply reflects the extent of humanity's first and most far-reaching garden failure.

November 19

One of my freshmen, a student from Kenya, is writing his term paper on the concept of sin in African religion. When I sat down beside him in the library to check his notecards this morning, I discovered he had turned up some fascinating material. His first notecard read:

> Sin is seen to be rooted in personal ontology. For example, when someone sins, it is to identify himself with sinfulness.

His second card read:

> Sin has psychic effects on another person. Sin is the attitude of heart and mind which spoils the life of another, especially of the family.

I was so excited by the subtlety of the ideas in these notes, a subtlety that far surpasses the old "missing the mark" definition I learned in catechism class, that I grabbed his cards and copied them so I could think about them later. This evening I find them as subtle as I did this afternoon. They contain everything necessary to understanding sin—an identification with Satan rather than Christ and the resulting broken relationships in the human sphere. Even the order is accurate. First, a disruption in the spiritual life of the individual. Second, a disruption in the social life of the human family. And third (my extension), a disruption in the relationship of the human to nonhuman.

November 21

I do not like hearing the 103rd psalm read in public. Though nearly twelve years have passed since I read it to Linda as she faded from consciousness the day of her stroke, hearing it brings those moments back so strongly I tremble. I know remembering is good. It is sound to recall how the Lord has delivered and preserved. But

I cannot remember without facing the awfulness: he also permitted.

November 23

While digging through the attic, trying to find *Great Expectations* for Melissa, I found a sketchy journal I kept in the fall of 1974 through the spring of 1975. I was worried about questions of identity. And more worried that I was worried. I thought I should have left them with my adolescence. Since then I've learned that life is a continuing identity crisis, that a person in the process of becoming a new creature in Christ is never completed. What one is today, one will not be tomorrow.

A few years ago when I spent that sabbatical semester in Kentucky, I often tuned in a radio evangelist while making my twice-a-week trek between Lexington and Louisville. I had little sympathy with his mixture of the gospel, free-enterprise economics, and anti-communism, but I enjoyed the exuberance of his rhetoric. One afternoon, near Frankfort, the sudden realization that we were brothers in Christ shattered my amusement. Though I probably could not hold a civil conversation with him, we'd be spending eternity together. Mark Twain's quip, "Heaven for climate, Hell for society," popped into my mind, and I took momentary comfort in the thought that the evangelist would be as uncomfortable in my company as I'd be in his.

Then I started to think: neither of us will have to tolerate the other as he is now. We will both be made new. Only those parts of us perfected by Christ will remain, and we will bear little resemblance to our current worldly selves. I can't imagine better news.

November 25

Though I seek to want
no more than I need

and turn my back
on the blandishments
of desire,
wholeness
is not mine.

Rumors of war
disturb my sleep,
and fears
of the end
of all life gnaw
my joy.

I live by moments
of vision
clearing
in the dailiness
of toil.

This morning
when I came in
wet with good sweat
from splitting wood,
the aroma of thanksgiving
played in the laughter
of mother, wife,
and daughter.

December 2

Though the weather remains unseasonably warm—near sixty today—granting us a reprieve from the cold, the fall is turning to winter. Nights are longer, it's dark when I waken, and dark when I come home from work. Except for bringing wood to the house, the outdoor tasks are finished, and I turn more and more to my students. I want to write about them, to show concretely how they enrich my life, to show how my work with them is one with my work in the woods and in the garden, but I have not learned how to temper my garrulousness for the sake of their privacy. So I write less of them than they deserve.

Early one afternoon before Thanksgiving I spent an hour talking to a fellow suffering from loneliness. Apart from allowing him to feel someone valued him enough to listen, I could do little for him. When I sat before my notebook that night, I wanted to get down my sense of helplessness before his plight; I wanted to get down the exhaustion and restoration I simultaneously experience in those situations. I wanted to say how giving brings unsought returns. But that night, caught up in the particular, I could not speak abstractly as I can tonight. Indeed, I did not want to.

I left the student out of my entry altogether and wrote instead of hauling manure and the stewardship of the garden. Now as I write, the relationship between the two parts of the day is coming clear. My responsibility to my student and to my garden is the same responsibility. My caring for the earth, without ceasing to be important for its own sake, is an image of my caring for people. I learn one by doing the other. Wholeness will come to me when I cease to know them separately.

December 5

In *The Climate of Monastic Prayer*, a book written relatively early in his life but published just before his death, Thomas Merton wrote, "One has begun to know the meaning of contemplation when he intuitively and spontaneously seeks the dark and unknown path of aridity in preference to every other." Something in me responds to that passage and says, "Yes, that's the way it is." For though I make my way by words, perhaps because I make my way by words, I distrust words. It's not my inability to manipulate them I distrust; I have felt on occasion the power to make them do whatever I want. It's the words themselves I distrust, their adequacy to comprehend the world. In the darkness of that doubt the way of negation and silence seems to be the way of hope.

Yet my attraction to this way frightens me. What spirituality I know is shallow. I have never been a man of prayer and probably never will be. I learned that several years ago when I made a retreat at the abbey of Our Lady of Gethsemani in Kentucky. Like my father before me, I tend naturally to the Saturday morning work crew not the Wednesday evening service. To approach this way casually, to flirt with it in poems extolling "Nothing" is to plunge not into the abyss of God's unknowableness but into the abyss of being unknown by God.

Two roads diverge in Dante's wood. I can travel only the one grace leads me down. Husband, father, poet, teacher, I am a man called to words and images, a man called to a worldly holiness, a perfectionism of knowing and being in the present. Grace points me to the way of affirmation.

December 14

Today is an anniversary we try not to remember. Twelve years ago, Linda's stroke knocked us out of the complacency of our youth into the companionship of imminent death. There had been a storm the night before, and deep snow, like the sterile whiteness of the hospital, covered the world. I remember too well the first night I sat up near her bed . . .

In the hall outside her room a stranger stopped me. "My mother just died," he said. I glanced vainly to the nurses' station for help, then turned my eyes to meet his. He did not meet them. His were desperate but ignorant of their desperation. I wondered what knowledge mine were giving away. My only words, "I'm sorry. My wife's dying," were unutterable. They would have hung in the air as meaningless to the stranger as his had been to me. They would have betrayed my will and loosed the fear I held knotted like a cramp in my gut.

I looked away and we parted. A few minutes later, an orderly wheeled a body past me, and I went back to waiting for Linda to stir. Every fifteen minutes a nurse disturbed my restless vigil. And each time, I felt my uselessness and irrelevance. I knew she wanted me to go home; I had overheard her saying so. But her annoyance had no power to move me. As long as Linda lay wordless in her paralyzed body, I would wait for her word.

The ancients associated the swift devastation of a stroke with the judgment of God. Modern medicine knows it for what it is. But Job's comforters persist. *God's gonna get ya for that* is a concept that survives in the caldron minds of many ministers who think the hospital the ideal place to preach their gospel of bad news. I put them out. God's word in the case of Linda's stroke was not the word of a hanging judge.

His word was *subacute bacterial endocarditis,* a debilitating word she had borne in her blood through the summer of 1970. In the fall, it spoke in her heart and settled in a valve. Two hundred and fifty-two shots of penicillin and streptomycin had laid it waste, but not before it had left her heart a traitor and her body vulnerable to its treachery. If we had been able to read the dumb abstractions of the medical report we had been given, we could have known and taken into our lives the grim possibility of what was to come; but we could not. The jargon slew us. We grasped only the fact that she was free of the hospital, free of the shots.

Still, one afternoon as we watched the onset of winter—an early snow streaked by red flashes of cardinal at the feeder—when Linda said to me, "You know, sometimes I think we're not through with this illness," I was frightened. Though I played down her remark, I remembered too well the September afternoon we'd prayed together. All summer she'd been listless and plagued by swollen ankles. Test followed test, yet diagnosis evaded the doctor. Finally he ordered a bone marrow, put Linda on tranquilizers, and confessed to me he was worried. We went home to wait out an anxious weekend.

Sunday, during Melissa's afternoon nap, we sat on our bed and talked. Slowly we worked our way to our fears. Then we prayed. And as we prayed I said, "Lord, we thank you for the work we know you are about to do." The words shocked us both. We looked at each other as the knowledge sank in. The months ahead were going to be difficult, but we had been given a gift of faith. We knew that when they were over, we would be together and Linda would be well.

That gift, hardly used during her endocarditis, loomed ominous when Linda voiced her premonition; I knew there was more to come. It came at 9:00 A.M., Monday, December 14.

Late risers then, we were just getting up. As she stood, Linda suddenly said, "Jack. Help. I'm dizzy." I eased her back onto the bed and held her hand as she was assaulted by Babel. Her speech slowly garbled; then everything crumbled. Her last clear words were, "Please. Read me the 103rd psalm." Until she could no longer follow I read,

> Bless the Lord, O my soul:
> and all that is within me,
> bless his holy name.
>
> Bless the Lord, O my soul,
> and forget not all his benefits:
>
> Who forgiveth all thine iniquities;
> who healeth all thy diseases;
>
> Who redeemeth thy life from destruction;
> who crowneth thee with lovingkindness
> and tender mercies.

It never occurred to me to ask what kind of mercies she was receiving; the statement was too close to irony.

What stunned me and silenced Linda did not surprise her doctors. They had found no sign of the embolism that had launched itself from her damaged heart, but they had known their fallibility before and knew the possibility of its presence. It fooled us all and left Linda isolated in pain and suffering. In an instant she had moved from the comfort and joy of our bedroom to the valley of the psalmist who walked in the shadow of death, and I could not walk with her.

She lived. But it was months of struggle.

The first Sunday she was able, we went to church. After the service, a friend, who had once been my teacher, greeted her. He spoke warmly, enthusiastically of her return. Then he stopped. The shining steel and plastic brace on her leg and the yellow wooden cane in her hand had caught his eye. "Linda," he said and wept.

It was almost three years before I wept. The necessity of Linda's recovery raged in me throughout her days in the hospital. The awareness of that Sunday-afternoon prayer sustained me. But along with that awareness I held to something less than graceful. Taking the conclusion of the book of Job to be roughly, "Shut up. What do you know?" I determined to endure without seeking to understand.

What saved me was the Proustian effect of a popular ballad about Snoopy's Christmas encounter with the nobility of the Red Baron. I heard it regularly as I drove the hilly roads between Houghton and Buffalo where Linda waited. I didn't think as I drove. I allowed the steady prattle of the radio and the humming of the snow tires to settle me into the warm void of the car. The drive was often pleasantly lonely. Roof-high snowdrifts isolated me from the landscape, then gave way to sudden openings on dazzling fields of crystal sunlight. The ballad operated the same way. The narration of Snoopy's danger—his guns out, the Red Baron on his tail—was both sentimental enough to move me and corny enough to make me laugh. It closed me into my own response. But in the chorus, accompanying the Red Baron's act of mercy, bells as clear and sharp as the sunlight cut through my solitude like the near irony of the 103rd psalm. Every time I heard them, my eyes clouded and I drove a little faster.

When the Christmas season ended and Linda came home, I forgot the ballad, the bells, and the sunlight. I did my best to forget everything. Three years later, as we were packing for a Christmas visit to our parents, I turned on the radio; Snoopy and the Red Baron were still in the air over France, and the bells . . . the bells were clear and precise. And the sunlight . . . the sunlight on the New York hills dazzled my senses. And all the fears that I had clutched and nurtured since the embolism spoke its bitter word poured out and ran away.

Linda didn't know what was happening, and I couldn't explain. How could I say that the bells in that silly song about mercy and joy and peace had become my madeleine and that I had just eaten the past like a sacrament?

And then I was laughing.

December 20

I am driving route 19 approaching Christmas.
The summer white farmhouses
Stand dull, grayed by winter's snow;
Their porches droop like hungry children
Tired after a day in school.
There is so much poverty.
I think *Even I am poor.*
But my life denies it,
Will not let my lips
Shape themselves around the lie.
On the seat beside me I have good gifts
For my wife and child,
And in my notebooks poems tilled
As jealously as the soil of this valley.
I have bound myself by words
And prosper in belonging.

WINTER

Let the snow fall this night
and cover our sins against the world

Let the scars of our restless flight
from nothing to nowhere
be iced and closed.

Let the wires of our false security
be weighted to breaking
and the lamps of our burning earth
be darkened.

Let nothing remain
in the emptiness of our hearts
but the dark of need

In that dark
let one star shine,

And grant us grace to spring
in the quickening light
it angles at creation

Winter has finally arrived. Eight inches of snow fell in the snow belt a few miles northwest of us. We'll get ours. We always do. When Lake Erie freezes over, the snows sweep further inland. When they do, and when the wind blows, the four mile stretch of Route 19 between Houghton and Fillmore, between work and home, becomes fearsome. Whiteouts are common. One minute my way is clear. A minute later it is obscure and dangerous. If there were a way to anticipate the sudden losses of vision, I could journey home in safety. But the whiteouts come with gusts of wind and allow for no preparation. They come like the sudden moments of alienation when one fears he is alone in a cold, hostile universe.

January 15

Snow fell during the night. When I went out at 9:30 this morning, the roads were still covered and slippery. I drove up the hill to the woodlot, parked beside the ditch I slid into last winter, got out of the car, and entered the woods. Blue jays shrieked at me from the trees but stayed out of sight. Before I'd gone twenty paces, they fell silent. Raspberry briars stuck like twists of old fence wire from the snow. They tore at my legs as I pushed through, but my pants and thermal underwear proved too thick for their thorns.

Nothing stirred. I walked in the crunch of my felt pacs and in the swish of my wool shirt against my vest. When I stopped, I could hear the wisps of snow falling from the overloaded branches to the woods floor. Far in the distance I could hear the cacophonous music of a flock of crows.

I had come to see the woods in winter, to enjoy a morning apart from the rush of a new semester. But as I worked along the east line of the woodlot, the glare from the snow, a painful brightness I had not expected on an overcast day, gave me vertigo. I could look at nothing close to me. I had to look far ahead to stay upright, so I walked almost unaware of where I actually was. Focusing on distant items, I saw a rick of poplar the community services work crew had missed. I saw a half cord of shagbark hickory we had missed. Its attention diverted from the present, my mind began to wander into the future. The nature of my walk began to change; I began to imagine and plan next summer's work.

A small swamp occupies the hollow between the woods and the meadow halfway back on our land. The swamp wasn't frozen, so rather than wade it, I went out onto the abandoned railroad bed when I reached its shore. From there I saw the meadow.

My mood changed abruptly. My desultory planning ended. Anger rose in me like a meltwater flood sweeping everything before it.

The crew that had taken up the railroad ties had used the

meadow for a turnaround. They had bulldozed the drainage ditch between it and the bed and had pushed gravel far up the slope of the field. They had uprooted four apple trees and shoved them in a heap against another. They had not used the meadow, they had abused it. And that was not all. Their abuse had invited further abuse. Someone else had used the crossing they had made to gain access to the woods beyond ours. Again and again, knowing no limitations other than the limitations of their machines, they had driven a large tractor across the wet meadow, rutting it deeply and irreparably everywhere they had gone. They had apparently gotten stuck several times for there were several sets of ruts.

The remainder of my walk was an inspection tour. I checked every possible point of access for damage, every grove for fresh-cut trees. Finding no other violations, I had begun to relax when I found the first posted sign we hadn't put up. I found one every hundred yards for a third of a mile. At every sign I grew a little angrier. At every sign I picked up my pace. I began to sweat, and I wished I had worn fewer clothes. And I worried, for I knew that before the day was over I would have to confront people I didn't want to confront.

The noise of the crows rose to a crescendo as I neared the end of our woods and the last of the interloper's signs, but I hardly noticed. As far as I was concerned, they were the avian kin of the human vultures who had violated the meadow and woods. Suddenly a loud clatter shook the brush near me. I turned, expecting a deer. A great red-shouldered hawk appeared, rising through the skeletal branches of the winter oaks, and I understood the unholy congregation of crows. I also understood, for the first time, Robinson Jeffers' terrifying line in "Hurt Hawks":

> I'd sooner kill a man, except for the penalties, than a
> hawk.

January 16

The anger I felt yesterday frightens me. I would like to say that the words I wrote were rhetorical, mere venting of tension, but I'm not sure that would be entirely honest. Jeffers was a misanthrope, and I said I understood him. I didn't mean that rhetorically. Rather than wheedle out of what I said, I must face the force of my feelings and my words.

Expressing anger as I did does more than release tension. It creates a state of mind in which violence becomes a possibility, for words shape thoughts and desires just as thoughts and desires shape words. This, I think, is what is happening in the United States as day after day newspapers carry stories about being prepared to fight and win a protracted nuclear war. If the talk goes on long enough, we will begin to believe it. We will become inured to the incomprehensible horror and immorality of it, and we will come to accept it as a harsh reality necessary to the preservation of "our way of life." It will, in fact, become "our way of life." Already it is being intimated that objections to using nuclear weapons rise from fear and lack of national will. At least two writers have argued in the popular press that nuclear weapons are God's gift to the white minority given to offset the yellow hordes of the east.

This morning, before anyone else was up, I read the account of Gideon's campaign against the Amorites. God reduced Gideon's army to three hundred men so the Israelites would be forced to recognize that the victory they won was accomplished not by the power of their arms, but by the power of the Lord. When will Christians begin to apply the clear lesson of scripture, turn away from trusting the power of men, and begin to trust the faithfulness of the Lord?

January 17

Several years ago I heard Wallace Stegner suggest that being able to distinguish between the time to apply a kiss on the forehead and the time to apply a kick to the seat was the most conclusive mark of a good teacher. If he is right, my teaching is going downhill, for I find it increasingly difficult to know which is called for. When I started teaching, I was all for kicking. My students may have been bruised, but I was sure they were tough. After about five years in the classroom, I began to have my doubts. Perhaps they were merely bruised. I stopped drawing garbage cans beside their bad sentences and started making ambiguous little arrows that mean "something is not quite right here, but I think you might have the idea." Lately I've been tempted to write, "Come on. Please don't break my heart by writing so badly I can't ignore your errors. Don't you realize how much I want to pass you?" I'm growing soft and wishy-washy.

The truth is I'm aging, and every one of my students looks like my daughter or one of her friends.

I think I can put this in more professional terms. Last week at an academic convocation, President Chamberlain spoke on what he called servant leadership. He distinguished between the prophetic and pastoral roles of the college. Both, he argued, are necessary. He implied that it is unlikely any individual faculty member can successfully perform both roles. In Stegner's terms, some faculty are called to kiss foreheads, others are called to kick seats. We complement each other. I'm in transition.

January 20

The third morning in a row below zero. The pipes in the shed room are frozen. Linda can do no wash until a thaw.

The creeks are frozen. A few more days of this solid cold and the river will freeze. I'd like to drive the back road, poke along the river on my way to work, but the state closed Lattice Bridge last summer, making it impossible to cross over anywhere near Houghton. So I will take the main road and barrel oblivious over the face of the earth as usual.

When the back road was open to me, I'd sometimes park and walk out onto the frozen river. Standing there, the summer landmarks, usually viewed from the canoe, softened by snow and transformed by my standing perspective, I discovered the valley made new. It was as if I walked in a lightscape.

> This river undercuts
> the banks that hold
> my thought within
> a stable channel;
> it once reached out
> and blessed my house
> with water.
>
> In sunlight
> I walk a winter way
> one side of sliding
> upon a will
> I can't by strength
> or words
> stay.

As serendipity, that experience is gone. As something planned, it never was. I'll not drive deliberately to the river to see the ice.

January 21

Below zero again. So cold the thermometer registers only a red puddle on the floor. My mustache froze when I went out to feed the rabbits. But there is a bright side. The day is brilliant, and the chickadees have found the bird feeder Linda gave me for Christmas.

* * *

As we were getting ready to come to campus this morning, I read Linda a paragraph from Frances Fitzgerald's introduction to her father's letters. When I read, "I have the impression that the only people quite as insufferable as writers are painters," I got the laugh I expected. I also got the mocking compliment, "You're not as insufferable as some painters I know." The joke was over, and I thought I was done with the sentence. But as I drove to my office, I began to think seriously, "Do I think of myself as a writer?"

I remembered Elliott Coleman coming into class one day just after being interviewed by a newspaper reporter. He had been asked, "Mr. Coleman, do you think of yourself primarily as a writer or as a teacher?" He slapped his knee and roared with laughter when he told us, "I said to him, 'Primarily I don't think of myself.'"

Though he was joking (humility required it to be a joke), Elliott was right. I'm not going to suggest that I don't think of myself. But I can say in my best moments I don't think of myself as a writer or as a teacher; I think of myself as a resident in a community that includes not only my colleagues, my students, and my neighbors, but the trees, the flowers, the birds, and the animals of the world around me. In that community I do things. I teach. I write. I garden.

Thinking of myself as resident makes clear to me the nature of the things I do, for thinking of myself as resident defines my relationship and my responsibility to the community. The things I do are functions of who and what I am.

January 24

The lousy, misbehaving mutt that calls me master took off last night when I let him out for his run. Periodically I went to the door and whistled for him, but he was gone. Coon hounds are by nature creatures of night runs and eerie music. At midnight I gave up, propped the door open, and went to bed. This morning I found him curled up on his mattress, innocent as can be, Prodigal Poon come home for his scraps from the breakfast table.

* * *

In my dream it was winter, and it was dark. Melissa was only five or six. We were leaving the grocery store. I was pushing the cart across the icy parking lot. Melissa lingered to play with the automatic doors. I called to her. As she turned and started to run toward me, a car careened into the lot. Its headlights struck her face, and I saw in her eyes the terror of a white-tailed deer frozen on the highway. The driver of the mad car never braked. My voice rose, a wild, animal scream, for it was all that could reach her. She fell.

The car passed over her and disappeared into the wall of the store. She jumped from the pavement and ran to my arms. I woke.

I did not want to go back to sleep, so I got up and wrote down the dream. This morning I showed it to Lionel. "It's a dream about grace," he said. Seeing my puzzled expression, he went on. "You could do nothing to save her. It was beyond you. Yet she was spared—spared in an impossible way."

Even as I write this, I find it hard to think that that awful image was a vision of grace. Yet I know it is true. What I dreamed is what Charles Williams calls "a terrible good."

* * *

What I saw when I looked out the window on rising this morning was not a terrible good. But it was good. Fifteen goldfinches, flashing in the sunlight, turned the air around the feeder into a dazzle of delight. As I watched, they were joined by a pair of purple finches and a downy woodpecker.

January 26

Christian Life Emphasis Week. The church choir, of which Linda is a member, sang in the service tonight. Consequently I was there. The text was, "A man shall leave his father and mother, and cleave unto his wife. And the two shall become one flesh." Usually messages on such texts delivered to an auditorium full of students send me off to daydreams, but tonight a little twist in the talk caught my imagination. I listened to the whole thing.

What got me was the frank admission of the complexity involved in balancing the injunction to leave parents with the injunction to honor parents. I had a hard time with that in my late adolescence and early adulthood. Strangely, though my father has been dead seven years, I am still learning what it means to honor him. In many ways, and I am convinced this is not fantasy or sentimentality, I am closer to him now than when he was alive; the communion of the saints is real and can be known.

* * *

The fall after my tenth birthday I began to take trumpet lessons. My teacher was an impatient man who'd stomp around the back room of the music store where he taught clasping his ears and muttering, "Oh, my God, my God," as I played. At home the reaction to my glorious noise was less dramatic. It usually amounted to the admonition, "Get back in there and practice." As Christmas approached, however, my father began to spend more and more time in the basement. I wondered if he wasn't feeling the same anguish my music teacher felt, but each time I visited him, I found him quietly fitting together small pieces of white pine. He refused to say what he was making, and I could not tell what it was, but he impressed me with the way he worked. Though his hands were quick and sure—the clean wood curled in amazing spirals from his plane—he did not rush. Time seemed unimportant, almost nonexistent. What mattered was the smoothness of the wood and the perfection of the fit.

Christmas morning I learned what it was I had watched him make. Beside the tree, holding my music book, was a wooden music stand more carefully shaped than any note I would ever play.

That music stand was a small thing compared with the work my father gave his life to. Shortly after crafting it, he and my mother picked out and bought four treeless acres twenty miles outside of Pittsburgh. Then working long evenings and weekends, they began the slow discipline of building a place worthy of the word "home." I was old enough to help, and I learned in aching arms and legs the weight of the gravel that lies underneath the concrete slab the house rests on. I learned the weight of the studs, the celotex, and the plywood. I learned how many nails go into the side of a house. With each wheelbarrow load of gravel, with each sheet of celotex or plywood, with each driven nail, I learned the cost and the pleasure of making a shelter from the weather. It was a good lesson, one I consider and cherish everyday as I go about maintaining and improving the house I have come to. But that is only part of what I learned.

The house, as it was built, was a glaring construction stuck by aliens on the surface of a field so long neglected that the alfalfa growing on it was good only for mulch hay and bedding. The house had to become more than a house; it had to become a place at once on and in the field. The long process of growing into and being accepted by the land began.

One Friday morning, about two years after my father died and I was home visiting my mother, I walked outside and stood on the back patio. A pair of black-capped chickadees scratched in the circle of sunflower seeds spilled under the feeder. No other birds would tolerate my closeness, but I knew, even in their absence, the squabbling jays and voracious grosbeaks that had spilled the seeds. I knew the hummingbirds that sought out the Joseph's Coat, and the maligned starlings and grackles that sparkled purple and blue and green in the sun. Down the bank from the feeder I could see the fishpond we had dug. Its water was dark and acid from the leaves that had fallen from the maple, now forty feet high, we had planted as a sapling years before. I went down the bank, past the pond, and across the lawn toward the forsythia hedge and the gate to the pasture. The lawn where we had played ball was thick with trees: small maples, evergreens, walnuts, and ornamentals I cannot name. Just before I reached the hedge, I stopped. At my feet was the feeder where my father had set out cracked corn for the pheasants. I remembered looking out the windows on winter mornings and seeing ringnecks and hens clustered like barnyard fowl around the corn. I remembered the pleasure my father took in drawing them to the yard. Raising my eyes, I looked through the hedge and over the gate to where he had kept a salt block to attract deer. It was gone.

I went through the gate, and the ghosts of Brutus, the big grey gelding, and Chico, the small, brilliant Arabian palomino, cantered up to me for carrots and conversation. Suddenly two deer exploded, white tails flashing, from the brush beyond the barn and bolted up the hill. They paused near the top, turned to look, then disappeared over the crest into the woods. I turned and walked back to the house.

By the time I got there, I was thinking of my father's life as an example of wholeness, of what a man by conscious effort might become. And I gave myself to the same pursuit of holiness he had given himself to, a holiness that would be worked out in terms of devotion, faithfulness, and craft.

Many times since then I've wished my father were around to see or to share something I've done. In those moments I realize my continuing need for his approval. I believe in his wholeness, but I know he did not achieve it consciously. He was not a man who thought that way. Nor did he rely on words to articulate his place in the world. Neither was he a good teacher. A consummate craftsman, he had no patience with the bumbling efforts of an

105

unsure beginner. What I learned from him, I learned from a distance. I watched what he did and imitated him when he didn't appear to be looking. But I think I knew then, as I know now, that he always was.

> The Sunday night he died
> I slept beside my wife
> On the living room hide-a-bed.
> I dreamed
> I slept where I slept.
>
> He came, dead but laughing,
> Into the room
> And shook me awake.
>
> I just want to be sure
> That you can handle it
> He said.
>
> Yes, I cried, I can
>
> Then woke myself screaming
> Go away!

This morning I recognize how much of my life, my concern with discipline, stewardship, and excellence, is rooted in a desire to prove to my father that I can, in fact, handle it. Not just handle it, but handle it with care and distinction.

I left home long ago. I married and made my exit plain. But the honoring involved in admitting my dependence on the example set for me goes on.

February 1

February is often the coldest month of the year. It blew in last night without its usual bluster, and the long-range forecast is for warmer temperatures than usual. I don't much care either way, for I'm always an optimist at the beginning of this month. When I turn over the calendar and see FEBRUARY at the top of the page, no matter how it might be storming outside, I believe in Spring. Though the days are lengthening, I doubt if this foolish faith of mine has anything to do with the actual cycle of the year. Instead, I think it has to do with the passing of my wedding anniversary at the end of January.

Seventeen years ago Linda and I were married. The pomp and rhetoric that overwhelm a wedding day have their source in a continuing imaginative act begun long before the ceremony everyone sees. That act, in which two individuals see themselves making by choice one life, is the beginning of marriage. And if a marriage is to succeed, that act must be repeated daily until, as the wedding vows so solemnly announce, death parts the couple.

Linda and I met and began dating when we were in high school. Though hindsight reveals how what we were then has shaped what we are now, I do not believe I began to imagine a marriage until we had dated several years. I was too unformed, too insecure to sustain the conscious attention necessary to see the possible life in our relationship. I was thinking mostly about myself.

I wanted to be a writer, and I had no idea how to go about becoming one. The simple solution of sitting down and writing never occurred to me. It was the late fifties, and writers wore berets, drank expresso, and lived in the Village. Image was everything. I expect I became insufferable. I know I eventually became a very bad college student; I refused to fit into any structured situation. I was an artist, and I expected the world to adjust to me.

I dislike remembering those days. I dislike remembering myself a fool, and so I will let them go unrecorded. Through them, Linda was the only constant I knew. As steady as I was unsteady, she believed where I had doubts.

In the middle of my junior year of college I gave up. I took everything I had written, burned it, and quit school. I headed home in confusion, but I headed home with an embryonic vision of wholeness, for as I made my decision to leave I was reading a little pamphlet by Fritz Eichenberg called *Art and Faith*. I have it before me now, and I am still judged and challenged by the passage I marked then.

> Most of us have sold our freedom for a pseudo-security, a shaky, uneasy prosperity which lulls our conscience to sleep. . . .
>
> If the artist's work is his worship, if he earnestly desires to serve God and through Him, man, the artist will, in the end, achieve that peace of mind, that freedom of soul, that mastery of matter which will bring him to the foot of the cross. . . .
>
> The artist who wants to serve God will have to embrace poverty—unsung and unwanted in our pagan world. Yet, I think those are the happy ones, happy as only those can be who live an integrated life. . . .
>
> Call it accident or atonement, we can't escape the command to be our brother's keeper. . . . Life and Art cannot be separated. We are all responsible; we should be seriously concerned. Whatever the follies of modern art may be, we have helped to produce them; they are a mirror held before us. Let's face it. We have to mend our ways and try to bring order into chaos, piece the fragments together, become whole again, holy again.

I stayed out of school a year. I worked loading and unloading trucks. The work was hard, but I enjoyed it. Slowly I began to heal, and the vision began to grow. When I returned to school, I was a different man; I knew myself well enough to include others in my thoughts. I went back to school imagining a life with Linda; not just a life, but a certain kind of life. I know this is true because she saved the letter I wrote to her when I left. The accuracy of its contents astounds me as I read it now:

I expect the things I write will never bring much money. It is no matter. I have no selfish motives or wishes for gain.

As far as I can see today, I will teach in a college and try to be normal. I will love you and our children. We will have a good life—not affluent, but honorable and Christian. Whatever God will do with my poems will be done. I will write them as best I can and pray that they are acceptable to him. If they are, nothing else matters.

These are my ambitions, simple enough, but I think worthy. To love God and strive to maintain his standards and to love you as Christ loves us.

When we were married, I was still a student. I had nothing to offer Linda except my good intentions and my ambitions. To my dismay and continued wonder, she found them, and has continued to find them, enough. The day we married it was snowing. Hard. My first act as a married man was to shovel a rented car out of the snowdrift that had accumulated around it while we were occupied with the ceremony in the church.

Normally the drive from Pittsburgh, where we were married, to Houghton, where we would live, takes about five hours. That day it took over twelve. We wound without snow tires over the twisting roads through the Allegheny Mountains, weaving between and around skidding and stuck cars as if we were ordained to go in the snow. We were; the weight of our possessions held us to the road. Dark overtook us before we reached New York. As I hunched at the wheel, gazing into the dizzying hiss of white against the windshield, the drifts mounded up beside us. We knew the road only by the steady whir of the tires and the outline of power lines strung like channel markers in a dangerous strait.

We made it through because we had no choice. Snow glazed my coat and hair as I unloaded and hauled suitcases, boxes, and lamps up the outside stairway to the two-room apartment I had rented and prepared for the coming of my bride. I welcomed her to a living room with a kitchen along one wall and a bedroom without heat. In the weeks before the wedding I'd done what I could to turn the cold barrenness of the rooms into a refuge we could rest in. I'd painted, made some primitive furniture to fill in the gaps between the furnished pieces, and hung some paintings. Still, when I opened the door for her, I felt the makeshift inadequacy of my efforts.

The next morning I went out to the car and found the wind had blown so hard during the night it had driven snow through the weather-stripping around the windows and had drifted the front seat full. I brushed it clean, waited two days for the plows to open the road, and returned the car. Linda went to work, and I went to class.

It was an auspicious beginning for a marriage. But that is all it was.

I still wanted to be a writer. Both Linda and I knew the risk involved in that choice. When I graduated, we packed up everything we owned, loaded a friend's car, and drove to Baltimore. Within two days we'd found an apartment, spent all our savings on tuition for a semester in the Johns Hopkins University writing seminars, and settled in to find out if I could write.

We quickly established a routine. Each morning I walked Linda to the bus stop as she went off to work. Then I went back to the apartment and wrote until noon. I discovered that I could discipline myself, that in fact I worked best when I was my own taskmaster. That spring semester I wrote my first mature work, a long poem about my grandfather. In the writing of it I began to define the attitudes toward my work that I hold today. I also began to define my attitudes toward my marriage and my family. For as I wrote and thought about the family I'd grown up in, I also began to exist in my own. In a strange city, with no friends, Linda and I learned to be together. We became one person. Our work became one work. We began to share the task that I had found articulated in Eichenberg. We began the long discipline of bringing order to chaos, the long discipline of knowing and saying the complex web of relationships in which we live.

By the time I had my graduate degree, Linda was pregnant. By the time I'd accepted a teaching position at Houghton, we had a daughter. We were young, happy, and invulnerable. Two years later Linda had her stroke, and all the easy affirmations became hard. "Till death do us part" ceased to be something we once said. "Till death do us part" became a member of the family.

We learned that our end is in our beginning as much as our beginning is in our end.

February 2

Groundhog Day. Carl Sandburg once defined an expert as "a fool away from home." Recently one such fool set himself up as an expert on winter survival. "The first thing," he said, "is never complain." He didn't have to say anything else. By that single remark I knew he'd never lived in the country. Around here complaining about the weather is, if not an art, at least a competitive sport. Any morning I want I can go upstreet to the post office and overhear or, if I think I have the edge, engage in the following conversation:

"Cold one today."

"Yup."

"How cold at your place?"

"Oh, down there. How 'bout yours?"

"Pretty cold."

"How cold?"

Dejection in the voice, "Eleven below."

"No kiddin'." Triumph. "Fifteen below down my way."

What the expert doesn't understand is that ritualized complaining is a means of reveling in one's hardiness. It is a way of saying, "No matter how tough it is, I'm tougher." It is a roundabout way of entering into joy and affirming the goodness of life.

The expert didn't do much better with the other half of his message either. He said not to think ahead to spring. Obviously he doesn't garden. It may be cold out, but in my imagination I'm already planting peas and onions. If I linger in winter until spring bursts in a shower of forsythia, I can count on spending most of my time in the supermarket next fall.

The groundhog, a better prophet than the expert, tells me I have six weeks to get cracking.

February 4

I was offered a pair of ducks today. I wanted them so badly I could taste them. Then I went home and checked out what Gene Logsdon had to say. "If you have a pond, keep a pair." I don't.

February 10

Fifteen below this morning. The rabbits had frosted whiskers.

February 11

Below zero again this morning, but knowing the light is gaining on the dark makes it easy to take. The mailbox has been overloaded with seed catalogs, and we're knee-deep in planning the garden. I spend far more time thinking about it than necessary. Over the years I've followed a succession of legumes and brassicas, light and heavy feeders. Since my plot is small, 1700 square feet, I don't have much room for experimenting. But when the beds are still under mulch and snow, it makes little sense to resist dreaming. Workable ideas sometimes occur.

I started tying flies for spring fishing—white maribous for calicos at Silver Lake.

February 12

The wind howls through the maple beside the drive and falls on the house. As the gusts draw across the chimney, the fire huffs and sighs. Heating with wood, I've become familiar not only with fire but with wind. Both were present at Pentecost.

February 14

Three valentines are honored this day. Only one of them interests me. According to legend, Valentine was in jail awaiting execution. On the day of his death he appealed to his jailer's daughter. The appeal did him no good, but his signature, "Your Valentine," has become our greeting-card cliché. Love and blood mingle; we pledge ourselves in celebration of a martyrdom.

*   *   *

Some of us do. No one sent me a valentine. I found, instead, a note in my mail from one of my students telling me I was neglecting her and not giving her the help she needed. She told me she thinks of my office as a lion's den and herself as Daniel.

February 16

Always there is the circling back. I read seed catalogs just as I did at this time last year. The vernal equinox is a little over four weeks away. Trout season opens a little later. Then the peas go in. Round and round. Nothing is ever finished. Success one year is preparation for the next. But it is no guarantee. The one constant is the repetition of the tasks. We choose to make that repetition a cause for joy or despair.

The cold weather has come to an abrupt end. The temperatures are nearly balmy.

February 18

This morning when I went out to feed the rabbits, I heard spring peepers. I knew it was impossible, so I went out into the backyard to see if the mock orange had been taken over by a flock of birds. It hadn't. The peeping, however, surrounded me. Then, through the gap between two houses, I saw a tractor pulling a trailer load of wood up the highway. The peeping reached its loudest and began to fade. It moved up the highway. Not spring. A chirping bearing.

As the peeping died, I heard a lone cardinal calling from the top of a poplar—a year-round voice in the wilderness signifying nothing.

Still, by noon it was over 40 degrees. Driving home for lunch, I saw a dozen wild turkeys scratching in the stubble of last year's corn at the edge of town. I turned around and drove back to watch them. They were well back from the road; the distance between us, which made it possible for me to stop without spooking them, made observing them difficult. I wished I'd kept the binoculars in the car instead of hanging them on a peg in the back room. With their long necks stretching first to the ground and then poking into the air in skitterish vigil, the turkeys were at once comic and beautiful.

February 24

I've been down with the flu for three days, but I'm on the mend. All the time I was sick, the weather was springlike. Temperatures soared into the fifties, and Linda saw a flock of returning geese. But as I got better, and as my students left for the February break, the weather turned blustery and the snow started falling. Winter has reasserted herself and shaken every hope we may have been indulging for an early spring.

In spite of her, we are warm and comfortable inside. Linda made a huge pot of vegetable soup for supper. I ate eagerly, my

114

pleasure in my restored appetite unbounded. Poon cuddled up on the porch with the bone, and the rabbits cuddled up in the hutch with the cabbage trimmings.

I am glad to be free of my students for awhile. I am tired of young writers disguising their negativism and hiding it behind a mask of truth-saying. Though I tell them, again and again, that a writer chooses the truth he tells, they do not listen. I remember my rebellion, and I know that they must resist me, that they must find out what I tell them in the crucible of their own experience, but I am weary. For their rebellion calls into question the conclusions I have come to about my writing. It forces me to be always testing myself, and times come when I would like to rest, assured that I am doing right.

Last week, after class, one of my better students complimented me on the way I had handled the discussion of a badly imagined, badly written story. He concluded, "I'd sure hate to have to do that year after year." Suddenly I was a senior in college trying to choose between a literature or a writing graduate program. I was saying to Linda, "The one thing I don't want is to be forty years old facing twenty more years of trying to teach undergraduates to write poems."

Tonight, after fifteen years, facing thirty more, I know the truth of my fears. I also know that I have found joy and satisfaction in my teaching—enough to sustain me and give the lie to winter feelings. Against these moments, I hold moments like the one a few years ago when a student came to me at the end of a semester. He was nervous.

"I think I ought to tell you this," he began. I wondered what was coming. "When I started your class, I had no idea what you were getting at with your talk about writing, wholeness, and holiness. I thought you were off the wall." I nodded noncommittally, and he continued. "Anyway, as the semester went on I started to get it. And, (he swallowed) I just want you to know that I've become a Christian because of it."

Not very good at handling such moments, I swallowed, shook his hand, and said, "Good. I'm glad for you. Thanks for telling me."

Memories such as that confirm for me that I am right. Though some writers are called to penetrate the darkness of their sinful nature, I am not one of them. I do not need to go into myself, stir up the hornet's nest of my evilness for the sake of frightening poems. My calling is to say the truth of what, by grace, I am becoming. My calling is to say that in Christ I am being made new, that in Christ the whole earth is being redeemed.

March 1

Every spring the obvious surprises me. Four days ago it was 32 below zero. This afternoon it is pushing 40 above. The sun is out, the melt is running, and the river is rising. All of that I expect; though winter keeps coming back, it never lasts more than a few months. The same, of course, could be said of summer. Spring as a metaphor for resurrection is of limited use to the poet. Nature has a habit of being cyclical rather than linear. One can as easily read death from it.

What interests me today is my response to the upward dash of the mercury: I left the house this morning in shirt-sleeves. Granted I was also wearing a down vest, but the 28 degrees felt absolutely balmy. The effect was heightened when the Spring L.L. Bean catalog arrived in the mail. Bean's selection of trout flies is irresistible, and I'm checking the days until April 1. But that's another subject.

When the mercury dropped to 28 last fall, I ran shivering to zip the lining into my coat. The change in my attitude toward 28 degrees is, I'm sure, the result of something more than relativity; it is the result of the direction of the earth. In the fall I'm turned away from the sun. The days grow shorter. The night and the cold come on. I shudder at the chill of darkness and turn to my fire, the sun

116

I've captured to lighten the image of my face turned gray and dead. In the spring the earth inclines me toward the sun. The darkness shortens. Light and warmth return. The small fire I've burned is taken up in the great burning, and laboring in the garden, I turn dark, becoming one with light.

A nice image that. But like the image of resurrection, it is a cyclical image. By November my skin will have paled toward the gray I fear, and my small fire will again be licking at the cold. Still the sun/son play on words is deep in our language. One suggests the other. Jesus is the light of the world. We live in him as we live in the light of the sun. It is direction that counts. Twenty-eight degrees is not very warm—but if one is inclining toward the source, it is shirt-sleeve weather. While I was eating lunch at the Inn, the only restaurant in Houghton, a farmer at the next table looked hard at the sun and remarked, "Fifteen days and we could be at it." In the timelessness of eternity, it can be sooner than that.

March 2

Evening grosbeaks appeared at the large feeder on the woodpile today.

March 5

A heavy fog filled the valley. A mile up Snyder Hill where we turned onto the old roadbed from the highway, we were still closed in. The ladders, saws, and clippers rattled in the back of the truck as Brian and I bounced over the stone, through the cut, and out into the open by the meadow. The apple trees, grown up in suckers and burdened with deadwood after years of neglect, waited for us there. More than two hours passed as we worked, trimming and climbing, cutting deadwood, cutting suckers, cutting the unfruitful branches that shoot heavenward instead of sweeping gracefully to the earth, before the sun burned through and opened the valley to

117

our sight. Even then the fog never completely lifted. It only opened below us. All morning we could hear the gaggling of geese headed north. We never saw one.

The trees we pruned are the same ones I was watching go wild last spring. Time has shown me that though I may have enjoyed the analogy implicit in their deterioration, I could not enjoy the fact. I feel compelled to attempt their restoration.

> Behold these three years I come seeking fruit on this fig tree, and find none; cut it down; why cumbereth it the ground?
> And he answering said unto him, Lord let it alone this year also, till I shall dig about it, and dung it:
> And if it bear fruit, well; and if not, then after that thou shalt cut it down.

We pruned six trees. We started one other but found no promise in it, so we cut it down. Two others are clearly dead. We'll firewood them in August.

March 6

I didn't realize how sore I was from yesterday's work until I leaned over the chopping block to split some kindling after church this morning. I thought I was going to stay permanently bent. My shoulders and neck seem to be the stiffest parts of me. No wonder. Most of yesterday I spent looking up the length of the pole clipper or the saw at the branches I was cutting. Having grown root crops, brassicas, and bush beans for so long, I'm used to kneeling when I seek fruitfulness, not craning my neck looking into the heavens. Perhaps the kneeling and craning go together. That they turn out complementary seems appropriate.

118

Yesterday when I fed the rabbits and filled the bird feeders, I spread some sunflower seeds on the roof of the hutch, which is under the kitchen window. I wanted to see if I could lure the birds closer to the house. This morning I watched them work their way in to the feeders.

First came the blue jays. Martinets in their dress blues, they can command the feeder. But they cannot understand peace. They flash to the feeder, grab seeds, and retreat to high branches. They trust no one.

Grosbeaks came second. They materialized, one at a time in the maple, like a guerrilla band laying an ambush. Then they changed character. Once gathered, they acted like a flock of flighty chickens. The slightest motion or noise would set them off, and they would rise as a group, flopping and flapping, sending up a tremendous ruckus, before settling back down to feeding.

The grosbeaks found the seed on the hutch. A small female, faded almost green, made the discovery. Five other females joined her before one of the showy males ventured from the tree. His plunge must have startled the rabbits, for the hutch suddenly lurched, as it does when they dash about. The lurching startled the grosbeaks, and they exploded upward frightening the rest of the flock. Only the female that started it all did not fly. She sat on the hutch calmly opening a seed.

Reassured, the others returned. After several repeat performances, the rabbits got used to them. Before I stopped watching and went to breakfast, I counted sixteen grosbeaks under the window, not one of them more than three feet from my face.

The smaller birds, the ones that feed on the swinging feeder, are the ones that know peace. The chickadees, juncos, and nuthatches sit quietly and feed as if they have no cares. Years ago, when we lived by the woods in Houghton, the chickadees would land on my fingers and pick seeds from the palm of my hand. Perhaps these town birds will do the same.

* * *

Windless, with a threat of rain, the ground still damp from rain a night ago, today was perfect for burning off the leaf mulch in the garden. I fluffed it up in several places, wadded newspapers, and stuffed them under the leaves. In the center of the garden I laid a fire using the leftover scraps of bark I no longer need for kindling. Then I lit the bunch of them. The fires burned slowly, sending up clouds of pungent smoke. I worked around the garden, forking the leaves away from the fence, turning them into the fires. When only the center fire was left, I cleaned the garage, sweeping the old hay, wood chips, and bark into a pile that I loaded into the wheelbarrow and then dumped onto the blaze.

Rain started falling. Not enough to drive me in, hardly enough to get me wet, but enough to make the fire safe to leave while I went to a committee meeting on campus. When I returned an hour later, a fine pile of ash remained.

The garden is ready to work.

March 10

The rain turned to snow during the night. Melissa stood at the hall window this morning and groaned, "Do you see what it's done outside?" Her tone made clear what she thought of the development.

I like early and late-season snows. Early ones are beautiful because they are a change. They signal Christmas and recall memories of sledding and snowball fights. When they come, I still can't resist grabbing a handful of snow and letting fly at a phone pole or a friend. Late-season snows are beautiful because they are so fleeting. I know it will be months before I again see the loveliness of the yard turned white and hear the soft hiss of flakes falling in the night.

This snow is already doomed. Though the sun is not out, the frost is out of the ground; I can see places in the yard where it is melting from underneath. The slight slowing of spring it brings is good. We are ten weeks from being safely frost-free, and March apple blossoms are useless if they are frozen in April.

March 11

> Meltwater full, the river's silence
> defines the grinding of the rocks
> beneath its star filled calm.
>
> March snow whitens the softened bank
> my touch knows better than my sight.
> An early carp plunges from the sky
>
> at my feet then rises back
> into the darkness,
> stars passing through his body.
>
> They keep pace as I walk,
> plummeting 67,000 miles an hour,
> trusting myself to this murky way.

March 13

Most people can breed rabbits. We aren't most people. Still smarting from last winter's fiasco, we put Momma Rabbit (something tells me we were counting fryers before they were kindled when we started calling her that) in with Charlie. She beat him up. Confused and intimidated, he huddled in a corner. Every once in a while he'd get up his courage, venture out, and sniff at Momma. Every time he did, she stomped him.

Tasting the bitterness of defeat, I reached in to remove Momma. She bit me.

121

I removed Charlie and put him in what used to be Momma's hutch. Then, good literary man that I am, I went to my books. There I discovered that fat does won't breed. Momma is fat. Momma won't breed. Therefore Momma is going on a diet.

March 14

We saw *Ghandi* Saturday. On the way home Melissa asked, "Was I supposed to enjoy that?" She didn't expect an answer. The film stayed present in my imagination through a meeting of the Community Services Committee on Sunday. In that meeting we discussed the problem of bridging the gap between members of a unique, largely academic community and the life-long residents of New York's most impoverished county. Alan Keohane, a member of the church and an employee of the County Office for the Aging, told us we are the ones responsible for the gap. We are the ones who must close it.

Some members disagreed with him, arguing, "We aren't high and mighty. We're just ourselves. We're willing to get our hands dirty. But those people have to accept us just as we have to accept them." My head told me to join in on Alan's side, but I could hear myself mouthing the same stupid words I would have been disputing. I stayed quiet.

How our words reveal the way we fool ourselves! How the phrases we choose to announce our goodness betray our fine opinions of ourselves! "We're willing to get our hands dirty." We might as well say, "We the clean are willing (with certain limitations) to help you the dirty straighten up."

In the corner of the room I saw a small man in a loincloth. He was spinning. Though he said nothing, his presence judged me.

I am writing these words sitting in a velvet chair. The chair is on a wool rug. Behind it is a Japanese stereo. Beside it are shelves holding a thousand books. I'm wearing a shirt manufactured in Korea.

Christ "thought it not robbery to be equal with God: But made himself of no reputation, and took upon him the form of a servant . . ."

I want it both ways. No. The truth is, I want it my way. I want the world to look at me and say, "Look at Leax. So accomplished. Writer. Professor. And so humble. Look how he accepts his role as servant." I make myself sick.

Christ will have none of it. He wants me to give up role playing and be a servant.

March 18

Poon met me at the car when I got home for lunch. He stunk. The whole porch, where he'd been lounging, stunk. I grabbed a quick sandwich, left orders for Melissa to bathe the mutt when she got home, and went back to campus.

After class, I sat in my office with a girl who knows the meaning of grace but has trouble accepting it. She wants, as we all want, to be just a little bit better before she asks for it. She wants to be just a little deserving. As she talked, I saw Poon, foul-smelling, wagging his whole hind end in joy as I approached. A dumb beast, he understands grace. He knows, however much his bad habits annoy, I will not beat him for being a hound. He knows I will drag him to the back yard, turn on the hose, and wash him. Soaked and lathered, he will be humiliated; but cleansed, he will be allowed in the house.

I thought, "If we, acting in the image of God, can be gracious to a useless creature, how much more abundant must be the grace of God toward us."

My student knows Poon. She has sat in the living room and looked into his liquid brown eyes. She has been the victim of his constant pursuit of affection, of his unrelenting desire to be scratched. I told her what I was thinking. She laughed, and she went in grace.

SPRING

Equinox: Calendar Spring.

During the night, the rain turned to ice. This morning the world is crystal. Light plays from the branches of the trees, but the branches are broken, hanging cockeyed and ugly. The day is a confusion of beauty and destruction.

* * *

At midmorning the ice turned to snow. Huge flakes covered the ground within ten minutes. Now, late evening, the wind blows, banging the porch door, drawing the fire, causing it to rise and fall with a wild chuffing sound. The sky is still loaded. The forecast is for the heaviest snowfall of the year.

* * *

Early this semester one of my students wrote a short story that offended a number of his classmates. The protagonist of the story was a recent graduate of an evangelical college, a young man who professed to be a Christian. The young man, however, had an unusual talent for compromise and self-deception. Always knowing what he should do, he found ways to do what he wanted. At the climax of the story, drunk for the first time in his life, he tried to go to bed with a more-than-willing girl. He failed. His drunkenness preserved him. He fell to the floor in a stupor and dreamed he succeeded.

Passages of the story were coarse. I was prepared for some discussion from the class. I had, in fact, selected the story to provoke discussion. But I was not prepared for the indignation and anger directed, not only at the story, but at the author. As a result I have been thinking about the nature and the appeal of pornography. I've done no formal research; I've picked up a few magazines in the drug store, leafed through them, and returned them to the shelf, and I've thought, off and on, about the many stories, novels, and poems I've read over the last twenty-five years. I've come to the following conclusion.

Pornography, like escape literature, is designed to encourage a reader to identify with and experience vicariously the adventures of cardboard characters. Unlike escape literature, which can be varied and harmless, pornography is single-minded and vicious. The subject of pornography is dominance. Sex is not central; sex is merely the means of presenting the victimization essential to the pornographic thrill.

A forthright presentation of a sexual relationship with all its comedy, pathos, and joy would be too fully human to please the pornographic appetite, for a relationship involves mutuality, the submission of each partner to the needs of the other. This necessary submission is precisely what the pornographer denies. Contrary to our assumptions, the pornographer is not crude. He knows the reader, even while he is rebelling against his humanity, wants to think well of himself. Deception is required, and it is the subtlety of the deception that makes pornography so appealing and so pernicious.

In pornographic works, one unwilling character (usually a woman) is made to submit to the sexual advances of another. The use of force, whether physical or psychological, makes the act a rape, a plundering of the integrity of a human being. The pornographer's subtlety lies in his ability to disguise the nature of the experience he invites his reader to participate in.

The woman violated always finds pleasure in the violation. She is always, in fact, grateful and eager to submit to further violations. This lie, fostering a twisted sense of masculine force and feminine receptivity, so successfully masks the perversion that the reader begins to believe the fantasy; he begins to believe his desires are the other's desires; he begins to believe every denial of his desire is a provocation intended to stimulate him; he begins to believe he is

128

irresistible; he begins to believe there are no limits on his behavior. The consequences of such a fantasy are obvious.

Women live condemned to be victims. Men live condemned to be restless failures, always seeking to be something they cannot be. For both, life becomes a joyless rutting and groveling after forbidden pleasure. The tragic irony, of course, is that it is their own perversion that makes it forbidden.

My student's story was not pornographic. The irony built into the tone and into the action—one sin preventing another—focused the attentive reader's attention on the aberrant nature of the young man's behavior. He was not a sexual hero. He was a fool. Should anyone mistakenly identify with him, he would not experience sexual arousal. He would experience acute embarrassment and find himself the butt of a moral joke.

Two observations occur to me. First, too often we declare a work pornographic because we find its subject matter distasteful. We ought to be more discerning. No subject is by definition pornographic. Consider the biblical narrative of Lot's daughters. Second, our emphasis on the submissive woman without a corresponding emphasis on the submissive male is foolish and probably contributes to the cultural atmosphere in which pornography thrives.

March 22

The predicted blizzard did not materialize. Still, it is snowing, and the wind is howling like February.

March 23

Ten below zero at bedtime.

I woke about six this morning and heard the furnace running. I thought about getting up to stoke the stove, but I said to myself, "Phooey. The furnace hasn't been on since Christmas. Let it run." I went back to sleep. When I woke a few minutes later, different thoughts kept me awake.

Yesterday Alan called from the Office for the Aging. He needed help. One of the women he visits, a seventy-one-year-old widow who lives alone in a trailer, is out of oil, wood, and money. Could I get her some wood? In the hum of the furnace I wondered how she was greeting the morning.

Life is so easy for me. I accept the hard work of heating with wood because I believe my stewardship requires it. But I know that should I become ill or lazy, my bank account would permit me to turn up the gas. Should I choose to, I have the power to live oblivious to the seasons. That power segregates me from many of my neighbors. It sets me apart from the elderly poor, the widows and widowers on fixed incomes who face winter with fear, who wonder if they'll live until spring.

After class this afternoon, Ray Horst and I borrowed a pickup, loaded a facecord of wood, telephoned the lady, and set off to find her. Though she lived deep in the hills, her directions were good, and we found her without missing a turn. She was waiting to help unload. We persuaded her it wasn't necessary, and she disappeared inside. A few minutes later, just as we finished, she appeared in the doorway and announced, "Coffee's ready."

Over coffee and bread with marmalade, she told us about herself. She was from Rochester. She and her husband had put the trailer in as a retirement home. Before they could share it, he died of cancer. Seven years ago she'd moved in alone. As she talked, I looked around. The trailer, filled with photos and keepsakes, was well-kept and comfortable. Her stove, installed by her son, was a good one, attractive and safe. Her new dog, a nervous Irish Setter pup, hid behind it and would not be lured out. She said her dogs (there was a Collie also) were her company, but she admitted to a loneliness they couldn't fill. I was impressed by her self-sufficiency and dignity.

On the way out we split a week's worth of kindling and casually asked why she hadn't called Alan for help before she'd run out. "Oh," she said, "I thought there might be somebody who needed it more than I did, and I didn't want to take theirs." She was a pleasure to help.

Driving back, I asked Ray if he had seen the truck in the church lot while we were loading. I had recognized it as Claude's. Several years ago a group of us worked at Claude's house, and I had had coffee with him. The communion that day, however, was unlike the communion we'd just shared in the trailer.

Claude is a cripple. But he is dirty and hard to get along with. He is a know-it-all and is convinced his troubles are the fault of the stupid government. When he made coffee for me, he took a jar of Maxwell House instant and two cups from the shelf where he stored rat poison. When he opened a drawer for a spoon, I saw mouse droppings. I figured if Christ could turn water into wine, he could make swill safe, so I drank and we talked. Claude bragged to me how he had swindled his previous landlord to save the money to buy the house we were sitting in. I looked at his woodstove beside me. The stovepipe ran through the wall without a thimble; the door was gone and had been replaced by a sheet of tinfoil.

I told Ray about that day. He understood. How easy it is to help the attractive and grateful! How hard it is to help the ugly and surly! I don't like the Claudes of this world. The best I can do is put my likes aside and do what must be done. Christ, who loves perfectly, will in his good time perfect my attitude.

Palm Sunday. Alan came up to me after church with another call for help. The late cold is hurting people who thought they had it made. We spent the afternoon out in sleet loading another truck with wood.

April 1

I wake at 5:15 A.M., fifteen minutes before the alarm is set to go off. I am not surprised, for I have wakened several times during the night. But now that it is time to rise, I am tired. "There's no sense in being fanatical," I tell myself. I turn off the alarm and roll over.

Twenty minutes later I wake again. This time I get up, go out to the kitchen, and plug in the coffee pot I prepared last night. Poon hears me stirring and barks to be let in from the porch. Before he can wake anyone else, I chase him off for a run. The air is cold. A heavy frost covers the grass. The thermometer on the garage reads 10 degrees.

I go back in to dress: thermal underwear, flannel shirt, wool shirt, jeans, snowmobile socks, and felt pacs. I eat, drink a cup of coffee, and pour the rest of the pot into a thermos. Six A.M. I've taken my time, but I can't dawdle any longer. I put on my down vest, denim jacket, and watch cap, grab the thermos and go. The tackle box, spinning rod, and bait can are in the car.

At the bridge over the Wiscoy, eight or nine fishermen are stepping all over each other trying to fish the same hole. Their lines cover it like a net, and I wonder if I shouldn't turn around and go home. But I see no cars down the road, so I drive to my usual spot, park, and walk the edge of the cornfield to the big hole under the willow tree. One man is fishing it. The hole is long enough for three friends to fish, but I'm antisocial. I move on. Since the next hole is also being fished, I leave the stream, cut through the woods, and return to it around a bend. I come out on the inside curve of a bend that cuts deeply under a bank and overhanging trees. No one is in sight.

Warming my hands around a cup of coffee, I watch the water. Ice lines the edge where the stream is shallow. The still backwater behind me is frozen solid. A single mallard flaps a lazy loop over my head, quacks wildly, puts on the speed, and barrels off toward the dam a mile downstream.

I fish the pool from head to foot, drifting a worm slow and deep. Nothing. The day is early. The water is cold. The trout will be slow to strike. I start over. My worm is about halfway through its drift; my line has arced in the current and begun to drag. When I begin to reel, to straighten the line so the worm will drift naturally, the trout, fully committed to his hunger, strikes.

Hooked, he slices upstream. I hold steady, letting the rod tip turn him. I reel as he slashes back toward me. He leaps. Once. Twice. Three times. And begins to tire. His life thrumming in my fingers on the line, I bring him to shore. I raise the rod high into the air, keeping the tension on the line, as I bend, take him in my hand, and lift him from the water.

In New York the opening day of trout season and April Fools' Day are always the same. This year the two are also Good Friday. As I fish, I think about the foolishness of the gospel. As I warm myself, clutching the metal thermos mug, I think about the man in the Philippines who will have himself nailed on a cross for the fourth year in a row to attract the attention of his American father who will not acknowledge his paternity. Doesn't he understand that the Father must turn away when the Son is on the cross? Doesn't he understand abandonment is part of the theme?

An hour later when I head home, my hands are too cold to clean the trout, but I cannot permit him to flop about the car slowly asphyxiating; I crack him sharply against the door frame. His color, his brilliant spots, begin to fade before I can lay him on the floor. My hands warm as I drive, and I gut him at home before I go into the house.

After lunch all the stores in town close for the community church service. I have been to such services. I remember, as a child, being dragged to a different church every day of holy week to hear meditations on the seven last words. I remember feeling holy, as if I were participating in some great observance, until Friday when I had to hear three last words in a row—every one of them depressing and grim. Then I felt miserable. Easter morning never measured up to what it was supposed to be. The gloom of Friday was too strong. It was and is easier to believe Christ is dead.

To believe, to live in hope, I must work against the easy affirmations I am called to make; I go out into my garden. I rake the hay mulch aside to see what winter has wrought. The six inches of manure I spread in the fall have compacted to two inches of muck. It hasn't rotted as I planned. It doesn't matter. I take the spade and begin to turn it under. The soil, worked year after year, is loose and friable. Only the manure is wet, and the spading is easy. I turn the whole plot, picking up worms as I work.

Finished, I realize I have sweat through two shirts and have worn my calluses soft and tender. But I have not blistered. I stand, tired, in the pleasure of the labor. The soil is ready to receive the seed. It will be a sign of the resurrection that, as the days lengthen toward summer, I will husband against frost, worm, and ground-hog, just as I husband the seed of new life within me against doubt and fear.

In the evening it begins to rain. It is raining when I go to bed. In the dark I lay awake and think:

> This spring shower makes
> the sound of spilling grain
> each drop a seed
> to be ground into flour
> and baked into bread.
>
> It is the body of the Lord.

Inside the dark of early spring,
I trailed across the lane
and clambered up the ramp
behind Pap. As the door
swung open, yellow light
spilled, like cracked corn,
onto the yard. I stepped
through its welcome sweep
and followed Pap
into the chicken house it warmed.

Broody hens shifted and clucked
in their beds of straw,
and clamoring in the life
of an old lamp,
the new-fuzzed chicks
tossed their shrill *peep peep*
into the rising joy
of the Easter world.

For the past year I've gone alone to the woods early in each season and walked a portion of the wood lot. I've gone to learn the way they change. On each walk I've also learned how I change, how my mood affects what I see and what I think. This morning I broke with habit and made the walk with Brian. Our concerns were economic.

One day last week, Brian and Rich had gone up to cut poplar. When they finished, they walked out to the meadow and found huge ruts crisscrossing it. Though the ruts ran through the same area I'd discovered despoiled in January, it was clear they were fresh. They were also greatly enlarged. Angry, they thought they knew who to see. But as they stood there, a young fellow driving a large Oliver tractor pulled up and started through the meadow.

Neither Brian nor Rich is small. When they yelled for the fellow to stop, he stopped. They explained politely that it wasn't in his best interest to mess up our meadow. In the ensuing conversation they determined that the woods beyond ours were being logged. The owner of the woods hadn't bothered to tell the loggers they needed our permission to cross the meadow. Aware that he was in a fix—the meadow is the only convenient access to those woods, and he was liable for damages—the logger offered to repair the ruts and build a road for us if we'd allow him to continue skidding. Aware that we were in a fix—the ruts were too deep for us to repair, and a suit would cost more than it would gain—Brian and Rich agreed.

The conversation wasn't over, however; the logger was a bold fellow, an opportunist willing to take a shot at any passing dollar. He asked to buy some of our trees. Today Brian and I were walking to consider his offer.

Absent from the first meeting, I was to play the heavy, the partner reluctant to sell. The role came easily. I didn't like anything I saw at the meadow. The bank I'd planned to sow in rye grass was stacked with muddy logs. The ruts, filled with murky, knee-deep water, were worse than my most pessimistic imaginings. Big machinery allows a man to circumvent the natural limits of his strength. It allows him to enter the woods and work when they are wet with the year's new birth. It allows him to take what he wants when he wants it, and in the short run makes unnecessary the discipline of nurturing the source. The full strength of my opposition to the mindless application of technology rose in me. As we crossed the meadow toward the lumbered woods, Brian tried to temper it.

"I saw worse ruts than these repaired when I worked for Davey Tree," he said.

"Leveled, maybe," I thought, "but not restored, not for a lot longer than we have to live."

The damage to the woods was greater than the damage to the meadow. As we expected, they were rutted. They were rutted axle-deep. Caterpillar tracks showed where the ground was too soft for the tractor and it had been pulled out. Deep, wide tracks showed where the tractor and the Cat had been abandoned and a skidder brought in. Trees lay in all directions, tops crushing new growth. Standing trees, trees that should have been freed to grow, were barked, permanently damaged by the skidding logs. Brian and I stood silently.

Finally I said, "I don't care what he offers."

"Neither do I," Brian answered.

We went back to our woods and began to walk the line. The logger arrived to see if we would deal. I think he knew before we even started talking that we weren't interested. He looked at a few trees, made an offer he knew we wouldn't take, promised again to fix the meadow, and went off.

On our way out I spotted the first spring flowers, colt's foot, dandelion-like blossoms on the cinder banks of the roadbed. I also saw the dog bones under the oak, the bones I first saw two falls ago. Having money, not mutability, on my mind, I did not bother going close to contemplate their passing.

April 9

Nearly a month ago I wrote, "The garden is ready to work." It was, but I was being optimistic. Though spring may send advance notices, she simply doesn't come that early in western New York. This morning I got back to work. I pulled the front off the compost bin and stepped back to see how it had done over the winter. The large stalks from broccoli and Brussels sprouts were only partially rotted. A few ferns were still identifiable. And except for turning brown, the grapefruit rinds were unchanged. These few resistant items laid on a bed of grainy, finished humus. I took a handful of it, crumbled it in my hand, and wondered again that I could turn the wastes of my life into such richness.

I hauled fifteen loads of new soil to the garden, raked it evenly over the surface, spread three loads of rabbit manure and rotted hay on top of it, and then Rototilled it all in. Around 10:30 Linda brought coffee out and we sat on the deck, enjoying what we had already done and thinking about what we would yet do.

For the past couple of years we've planted peas and beans in succession, allowing us to grow twice the vegetables our plot would normally yield. Until last year when an August frost almost ruined the beans, our system worked well. Remembering that, and knowing what other summer work lies ahead, we have decided against succession planting this year. But as we sat on the deck with our coffee, casually discussing where we could put a blueberry hedge, an asparagus bed, and a small barn, I had second thoughts. The garden is not large enough to grow what we want without succession planting. Linda looked across the yard at an old flowerbed I've been despising for years and said, "I expect we'll never get that bed in shape. Why don't you till it under?"

I knew what it cost Linda to give up her dream of flowers, but the only guilt I felt pulling the starter rope on the tiller was for not feeling guilty. When I finished, Linda looked a bit mournful. "I'm sorry to see them gone," she said, "but I think it's important that the yard and garden be neat. It's part of our witness."

April 13

I've talked about peace. I've written about both its presence and its absence. Today I acted. I drove to Olean to meet with a priest, a nun, a Methodist minister, a college professor, and a poet to begin a discussion of what it means to be peacemakers here in the Southern Tier of New York.

We recognized that peacemaking is a radical activity, an

activity that is likely to face opposition. We accepted that possibility. But we were careful to define the nature of the peace we seek. Though peacemaking must take place in the political arena, the peace we seek is not political. It is not merely a cessation of intimidation and war. It is spiritual. It is coming together in harmony and communion. It is living in fellowship with all creation, human and nonhuman.

To make a beginning we have decided to sponsor a picnic for peace, Mayday on the Mountain, at Merton's Heart, a meadow overlooking the Allegheny River and the St. Bonaventure University campus where Thomas Merton taught before becoming a Trappist monk. We plan to share readings and food and simply gather with a few others who believe world peace is an extension of personal peace and neighborliness.

Our plan is simple, yet I am apprehensive. I am afraid that though I intend to bring about good, I am likely to bring about division. Many of my friends will support me. I'm counting on them to join me at the picnic. But I have other friends, Christians I respect, who argue that the only response power understands is power. Many of them have had military careers. Some of them scorn pacifists. One has said, "I went to Vietnam so you guys could march around protesting."

Though I am afraid of what I plan, I am convinced failing to do it would be a betrayal of all I have come to believe. My freshman Bible teacher said that bondage to sin does not necessarily mean being unable to choose good over evil. It sometimes means having to choose between two evils.

Reluctantly, after long thought, I have made my choice.

April 16

We no longer go to the dump. We go to a collection site, an elaborate artificial hill mounded around an immense compacter. We drive up the hill, unload our garbage into the covered bin, and pull away. Throughout the day, as the bin fills, the compacter does its work. Sometime in the night a truck backs under the bin, is coupled to it, and hauls it off to the Cuba Cheese factory where everything is incinerated and used as an energy source. It is truly wondrous, and in Melissa's words, "It doesn't even smell."

*　　*　　*

Blustery morning, half snow, half rain. Brian and I spent it working on the tractor. We changed the flat tire, the oil, the plugs, and we rewired the juryrigged ignition system. Next week we'll try to start it.

Around noon we went up to the wood lot to see what the loggers were up to. We found one, working alone, trying to wedge a tree and free his pinched saw. He couldn't, and we didn't have any tools with us, so we talked. Mostly we listened. The fellow, in his midtwenties, stood in a deep rut and said, "If'n it was me, I'da waited till summer to do this. Too much mud. But everybody, I guess, needs the money now. Know I do." He pointed to his Cat, spit, and went on, "I'm three payments back on that and two on my tractor. With that saw pinched—I ain't pinched a saw this whole job till jist now, the wind's come up—I ain't makin nothin."

For nearly half an hour, sitting on a muddy butt log pulled out onto the roadbed, we talked and waited for his partner who usually cuts firewood for a living to come back from his breakfast. He arrived on a little Ford tractor, which became the topic of conversation. Between the Ford and the skidder parked down the tracks the fellow had $32,000 invested in equipment.

Brian asked, "You're paying for that cutting firewood?"

"I'm trying."

April 18

Larry stopped by the office today. He's located this year's lamb, a Hampshire ram just ready to be weaned.

April 19

On my way to Olean for another Mayday on the Mountain planning session I drove through an area owned by Amish farmers. They were out with their horses plowing. Though they reject much technology, they do not reject technology. They are skilled, sophisticated laborers who have recognized, unlike most Americans, that technology must be used within boundaries set by cultural and moral understanding. Human nature is such that doing what can be done overrides the impulse to ask the limiting question: "What ought to be done?" The Amish have asked that question.

The mud-mired loggers beyond our wood lot are men who have not. They shouldn't be in the woods. They knew that the moment their tractor began to sink. They chose to ignore their moral obligation to respect the health of the forest. They brought in bigger equipment: tractor, Cat, skidder. With each escalation they increased their financial risk, making further escalations necessary. I cannot say with any assurance, given the need for cash and the power to act, that I would do any differently. But I have limited myself. The small tractor we use makes it impossible for us to even consider entering the woods. For the Amish and for us the right thing and the possible thing are the same. The moral choices we have made restrain our natures.

All of this is related to my drive to Olean and to Mayday on the Mountain. The weapons of war, our capacity for destruction, have outstripped our ability to restrain ourselves. The bomb has been dropped. Unless we act as individuals, as a nation, as a world community to limit the technology of death, unless we find the courage to say, "No matter what, this I will not do," and remove from ourselves the possibility of doing it, we will find the provocation our violent natures desire; we will destroy the world.

April 22

Momma Rabbit's diet seems to have been successful. Charlie bred her this morning.

April 26

The last planning session for Mayday is over. I wonder if anyone will come. What we're doing seems so small and silly.

I think our emphasis on striving for peace in our individual lives is right. Part of me would like to be more political—"Let's send Washington a message"—but as I examine my feelings toward those I've joined with in this effort, I recognize how fundamental I must be. I simply don't like one of them. He is the first person I've encountered who is offended by the Beatitudes. Probably I should admire him for recognizing how radical and offensive they are, but his objections challenge the security of my assumptions. I'd like to be for peace without him.

So. I come in my own person to the central issue: How do I love this man as myself?

May 1

Larry and I were the first in the parking lot at St. Bonaventure's. The day was overcast. Rain was imminent. It occurred to us that maybe no one else would come. But they did. They came in small groups, two or three at a time, tentatively, as if they weren't sure they wanted to be involved. Sister Kathy gave me a roll of white crepe paper, and I began to make armbands. I felt a bit unhinged, as if I didn't know the strange person going from marcher to marcher, touching each one, experiencing an uncanny intimacy as he pinned the band on each. I wasn't sure I wanted to know him.

A reporter from the *Olean Times Herald* roamed among us taking photographs. "Hold that a second, please. Got it. Thanks. Can you two stand a little closer? That's it. Good." Our self-consciousness neared embarrassment. We started walking.

As if the beginning of the march were a signal to the heavens, the rain let loose. It came down in sheets, drenching us before we walked the first block. A few marchers had umbrellas. A few had ponchos. One had a great canvas, which four held aloft by the corners while a half dozen walked under it. We looked a foolish lot of pilgrims. But we laughed.

Near the bridge over the spring-swollen Allegheny, the entire youth group of the local parish (some of them on bicycles) joined us. Led by a pretty young sister, they started singing, "This is the day that the Lord hath made." A better song might have been, "Oh, no, don't let the rain come down." But they seemed to be enjoying the fiasco. We all were.

As we crossed the bridge, the fire siren went off. The parish priest, in ballcap and yellow slicker, borrowed a bicycle and pedaled off to answer the call. Fifteen minutes later he was back. False alarm.

Our crepe-paper armbands turned transparent in the wet and began to fall from our arms. The rain soaked through our clothes and we began to feel the chill. We walked faster and covered the distance to the trail up the hill to Merton's Heart ahead of schedule. We stood around waiting for those who had not marched but planned to meet us for the ascent. Paul Robinson, minister of the First United Church of Christ, arrived and began passing out small green hearts to pin on our nonexistent armbands. The last of our mobile congregation arrived with him, and we started up.

The rain had turned the trail into a stream. We walked in an inch of water running over clay. Many slipped and fell. Where we had been merely wet before, we were now muddy. I abandoned the trail for the solid ground held in place by tree roots. I climbed. And I wondered what being cold and miserable had to do with peace. I wondered what my gesture meant to anyone.

When we finally reached the meadow, a steep, dishlike slope reminding me of a Greek amphitheatre, we divided ourselves into audience and readers. We stood facing up hill looking at the audience that looked down past us to the river and the city of Olean below. The rain continued to fall as we read, streaking the dittoed pages, obscuring our words.

Then we prayed.

Most gave up picnicking and fled for the cars waiting to take us back to town. A few sat in the drizzle and began to pass out fruit. A wine bottle appeared from the knapsack and began to circulate. Larry and I each accepted an apple, said our good-bys, and beat it down the hill. We didn't stop until we reached the closest Mr. Donut and a steaming cup of coffee.

Fifty people walked for peace. Fifty people got drenched and mud-caked. Several probably caught colds. A couple wound up with their pictures in the paper. Who did we influence? Most likely no one but ourselves.

Where else can we start?

May 2

When I went into the garage this afternoon, I heard a wild scraping and thrashing in the back corner where I keep rabbit food and birdseed. The racket was so loud I wasn't sure I wanted to investigate. But I didn't have to. Before I could move, a chipmunk burst from the bag of sunflower seeds, flipped head over tail onto the floor, and dashed to the safety of the woodpile.

A few minutes later I returned and was treated to a repeat performance. Enough was enough. I don't mind the little blighter stealing from the feeder, but I will not allow him to set up

144

housekeeping in the bank. I sealed the bag and moved it. I expect the birds will finish the seeds before he finds the bag and chews through it.

May 3

I have always liked rambling, loosely organized books that can be browsed randomly. Journals are perhaps the best of these. Thoreau's journal is perhaps the best of all. I don't have the whole thing, but I have multiple copies of selections from it. I keep one in my office and a couple of others around the house so I can dip into it, given an idle moment.

Today I opened it to March 15, 1852: "The air is a velvet cushion against which I press my ear. I go forth to do something in it worthy of it and of me . . . ." Thoreau at his best can be matched by no other writer. No one else so perfectly unites the sensuous and the ideal. No one else so perfectly expresses the double layer of experience. His achievement, however, involves risk. To avoid appearing a fool, he must always be at his best. He is not, of course, and when he misses, he misses spectacularly. He comes off sounding prudish and stuffy.

A few weeks after pressing his ear against that velvet cushion, he complains of a companion who made a joke about sex: "A companion can possess no worse quality than vulgarity. If I find that he is not habitually reverent of the fact of sex, I even I, will not associate with him. I will cast this first stone. . . ."

Imagine the sufferings of a woman whose husband is always reverent of the fact of sex. Such solemnity would make Planned Parenthood superfluous.

May 4

My garden has taught me to think ahead. For it to be fruitful, I must plan. I must build soil, plant, and nurture what I have

145

planted. It has also taught me to hold the harvest lightly. Over the course of a season I can lose a crop to spring rains that rot the seed, slugs that eat new shoots, rabbits that eat everything, hail that breaks the strong, and drought that withers the weak. I can lose a crop because of my ignorance or my carelessness. Until I have the fruit in storage, where it can also spoil, I live with uncertainty. I do my best, work faithfully, and hope.

Few moments in the garden are worse than those when I stand over a diseased or dead plant, admit that it is gone, reach down, pull it, and toss it on the compost pile.

Teaching is much like gardening. This morning I looked down on the work of two of my senior majors and found that it had withered. They had nothing to show. I flunked them.

As I walked across campus to turn in their grades, I wondered what I might have done to prevent their loss. I wondered if I had taught or if I had merely gone to class. I wondered whose failure I was reporting.

May 14

Coming home from class a week ago, I spotted a painted turtle on the highway. Because some idiots delight in squashing them on the pavement, and because I like turtles, I stopped and picked him (her?) up. For the moment I have him in an old cooler in the garage, and I am trying to decide whether I should set up the aquarium and keep him or turn him loose in the swamp. Though I have no real preference, I suspect the turtle does.

When we were boys, my brother, who is now a sculptor, wanted to be a herpetologist. I had no such ambitions, but the field fascinated me as well, and I was willing to help him with his collecting. The day came, however, when he strained my good nature. Not satisfied with the box turtles we found in the woods, he went out and bought a painted turtle slightly larger than the one

I'm currently keeping. All went well until he decided to let it have a swim in my fishpond.

I had dug the fishpond by hand, mixed the concrete for it, and poured the sides myself. I had planted the lily that lay in splendor on the surface, and I had stocked it with fancy goldfish. My goldfish were wonders. They were ornate finned flowers, multi-colored, fan-tailed, and lovely.

They could hardly swim.

The turtle, awkward and lumbering on land, was transformed when he slipped into the water. We could not catch him. He disappeared into the deepest water under the lily and waited. One after another my fantails swam too close to a mystery beyond their experience.

I replaced them with catfish and bluegills.

This morning Brian Reitnour, our five-year-old neighbor, called me at my office and asked where the turtle was. He wanted to feed it. Later, Linda told me what happened after he hung up.

She took him to the garage and told him to get a worm from the worm bed. He turned over the bedding and was just about to pick up a worm when he paused.

"Aunt Linda, do worms have mouths?"

"Yes."

"Do they have teeth?"

"I don't know. Not very big ones if they do."

"I think I don't want to feed the turtle."

* * *

Yesterday he was helping me with the yard work. Since my mother was on her way up from Pennsylvania for a visit, we were talking about mothers. I asked him if he thought old people needed mothers.

"Everyone has to have a mother," he said.

"What for?" I needled.

He looked at me as if I were the dumbest man in town and answered, "You got to have someone to love."

May 15

The maple beside the house is leafing, but it has not filled out yet. The sun shines through it and spills onto this page, dappling my words. The larch is green. The dogwood is in blossom. The peas are poking through the soil in the garden.

Last night we saw a hen turkey in the woods. I let the turtle loose in the peeper-filled swamp. Spring is on schedule.

* * *

Around 8 P.M. Willis picked me up and we went up to the dam at Mills Mills to see if we couldn't entice a couple of night-feeding brown trout to bite. We sat fishing in the soft glow of the Coleman lantern. In the mantel hiss I thought of the camp on the Allegheny where I fished with my father and his friends when I was a teenager. The quiet of those days and the quiet of the evening settled into me.

Linda tells me I don't know how to relax. She may be right. I often have a hard time distinguishing between the good things I'd like to do because my perfectionist nature tells me I ought to do them and the good things I must do because the Lord requires them of me. Adding task to task, imagining a perfect world, I demand more of myself than I can give. I get frustrated and then angry. God would be better glorified if I would allow him to perfect the world in his way in his time.

We'd fished about an hour when the wind came up. At first it rippled the surface of the water. Then it bent the trees. At last it howled down the valley, drowning out the sound of the water going over the dam. For half an hour the wind stormed, but it brought no rain. Then it died. The surface lay smooth again, and we sat in the rush of the spilling water.

May 16

I set out two dozen broccoli plants, a dozen cauliflower, and a dozen Brussels sprouts. I intercropped spinach in one of the broccoli beds.

May 17

We cut tops today. Putt, Rich's dog, sniffed out an opossum in one of the down oaks, cornered it, caught it, and with a quick shake of his head snapped its neck. "One less varmint," Rich drawled, but the tone of his voice revealed displeasure. Though Putt was only obeying his nature—if he weren't so well fed, he would have eaten it—and we had no cause to feel anything, we felt loss. Something had gone out of the world. We had felt another small death and taken another preparatory step toward comprehending a large one.

I remember how maturely Melissa, who was six at the time, responded to my father's death. I said to her, "Do you know what this means? You'll never see Papap again."

"Yes I will," she answered. "At the resurrection."

A few months later she wept inconsolably at the death of a pet hermit crab.

May 19

The circle of this year and of this journal is beginning to close. We went to Kelly Brothers Nursery with Bonnie and Larry for the annual half-price sale on bare rootstock. As it did last year, it rained. And as we did last year, we didn't make up our minds about what we would buy until we got there.

Larry wandered from bin to bin in that wonderfully musty

storeroom that smells like life rising from the ground, muttering, "A man planting trees is an optimist. A man planting trees . . ." Linda and I went about our usual good-natured dispute. She headed to the flowers and shrubs. I headed to the fruit trees. She thinks the ideal yard is beautiful. I think the beautiful yard is edible. She bought a forsythia. I bought two dwarf apple trees, MacIntosh this year, and five blueberry bushes.

Larry proved his optimism by purchasing a pie cherry, a tree he's lost two years in a row.

May 20

This morning I gave an exam. I passed it out, left the room to get a cup of coffee, returned, and sat down at a desk to write. One after another, students came to me with questions. I didn't write a word. Near the end of the exam period I happened to look at my hands. The lines in the forefinger and index finger of my right hand—except where my pen has polished a callous smooth—were filled with greenish dirt. In that dirt and that callous I see the marks of the conflict that plagues me every spring. The callous is from writing and marking papers. The green dirt is from squashing slugs in the garden before class.

This spring has been more difficult than usual. It has been as cold and wet as winter was warm and dry. I've done my outdoor work quickly, relying on habit, working without thought, and missing much of the pleasure I usually enjoy. Compounding the difficulty, I've been teaching a four-week May-term course I do not usually teach. In that work also I have rushed, and I have worked without proven habits to fall back on. Though the necessity of daily three-hour lectures has guaranteed my taking thought, I have not felt joy in my thinking. My mind wants to turn from the classroom, from thinking about the world, to being in the world. But it cannot. The class holds me back. And this journal holds me back. I am experiencing my life as material to be made into prose.

150

Though I realize this is the dilemma no artist resolves, I am not comforted.

*   *   *

After class Larry came by and suggested we haul the canoe up to Silver Lake to see if the panfish spawn has started. Since I keep the canoe behind the rabbit hutch, we stopped to see the rabbits. I showed Larry Poppa's skin problem, some sort of fungus infection that has me concerned, and then we checked out Momma, whose Christian name is Paksu. She was in her nesting box getting ready to kindle.

The panfish spawn hadn't started. The wind was blowing, pushing up whitecaps, making fishing impossible. That the fishing was bad didn't matter. The first day on the lake is always good. Pushing off from shore, moving from the stability, from the stolidity of the land to the lightness of the canoe on water, to the seeming unstable glide and slide in the wind and current, is liberating. All the thick-headedness caused by closed windows and stuffy rooms is blown away by the entry into the world of herons, gulls, and ducks. We paddled across the lake to a protected area, caught a few small perch, returned them to the water, and came home.

Melissa met us in the drive.

"Paksu is dead."

"What?"

"Paksu is dead." She spoke without expression.

I thought of Poppa's infection. "Poppa?"

"No. Paksu. Come see."

We went to the hutch, and there was Momma, stretched full length in the nesting box, cold and stiff. Still too fat, she'd had difficulty kindling, and no one had been around to help her.

Without ceremony we buried her in the garden. How matter-of-fact death becomes.

May 21

To plant the blueberries I had to dig a trench sixteen feet long, two feet wide, and two feet deep. The work was surprisingly easy; the soil was light and loose, filled with organic matter. The five years I've spent mulching, manuring, and cover cropping have paid off. I took the soil I'd mounded beside my digging, mixed it with peat moss to increase the acidity, and refilled the trench. Then with my hands I scooped out shallow holes for the spreading roots of the blueberries. I set the plants, pruned, mulched, and watered. In a few weeks I'll add a pine-needle mulch for acidity.

The soil I worked in was so friable it made me curious. I took a long stick and pushed it into the garden to see how deeply my mulching had worked. It went in two feet. I took the same stick into the middle of the yard and pushed much harder. It penetrated six inches.

June 5

Potatoes are supposed to go in on St. Patrick's Day. If I were serious about potatoes, I'd be behind, but this valley I live in is potato heaven. In the fall when the commercial growers harvest, we can buy all we want for less than $4.00 per hundred pounds. At that price I'd be nuts to dig my own. I plant my leftovers just for fun.

This year I probably wouldn't have bothered. I probably would have napped in the sun, except Brian Reitnour appeared at the door after lunch and announced, "Uncle Jack, I've come to help you work."

I asked him, "What work?"

And he answered, "Your garden. We've got to finish your garden."

I said good-by to my nap, got my shoes, and went out to the garage with him. He was quite indignant when I didn't give him a spade. "I can dig too," he said. "I have my own shovel at Papop's in Pennsylvania." I handed him the sack of sprouting potatoes to carry. "Umph, these are heavy," he said as he staggered across the yard. He was quiet as I dug a trench for them, cut them into sections, and placed them in the ground. But his patience wore out.

"When do I work?"

"Now." I gave him the shovel and told him to cover the potatoes. He labored mightily. The shovel was as big as he was, but he was determined. He did good work. I didn't have to do any of it over.

While he was occupied with the potatoes, I Rototilled a new section of garden so we could set out the tomatoes. The wind blowing through my hair felt good. But it also annoyed me. I went inside and got my hat. Brian put down his shovel, ran home, and came back in his. "This is my John Deere cap, Uncle Jack. My Papop gave it to me in Pennsylvania." It was brand-new-clean. He looked at the years-old, sweat-stained thing on my head and said, "Let's trade hats." I suggested his Papop probably wouldn't think much of my hat, and we went back to work.

I dug the tomato plot a little deeper than I could Rototill it, and Brian picked fishing worms from the clods until I was ready to set up the trellis. Since I sweat easier than Thoreau who claimed to have dug his cellar in an hour of easy work, I removed my shirt after I finished the first post hole. Brian followed suit. I let him fill and pack the holes as I set the posts, and I let him plant about half the tomatoes. Then I took advantage of his legs and sent him to the garage for the plastic jugs I use to protect the plants from frost. Carrying one jug at a time, he made two dozen trips before we were done. I got tired watching him.

153

When we quit, we sat on the deck. I had an iced tea. Brian had a glass of milk. He looked up at me, his white mustache outlining a grin. "Do you know why I help you?" he asked.

"No. Why?"

"Because God wants us to help one another."

"Do you know what happens when we help each other?" I asked.

"What?"

"Everyone's work gets easier."

Without speaking, I thought of the way the afternoon had gone. It wasn't literally true that he had made my work easier. He had, in fact, made it go a good deal slower than it might have if I'd worked alone. But then speed has never been a measure I've subscribed to. With him at my side, a child playing at work, I felt the element of play myself and worked once more in joy.

June 13

The panfish spawn is on. Two days ago, Roy and I put the canoe in at Mack's about 4 o'clock. We paddled straight to the logjam on the south shore, tied up to one of the logs, and never moved. It was 85 degrees out, but the action was so fast we forgot to eat, we forgot to drink. I was catching fish on flies I'd tied myself. By 9 we'd boated over 150 fish.

I was so thirsty when I got home I kept waking in the night and getting up to drink.

Last evening I went back with Larry. The fishing wasn't quite as fast. A wind had put them down. We only caught about 100. Of the total catch, I kept 40 fish, which I froze whole. I'll fillet them a meal at a time come winter.

When I went to sleep, I saw fish in my dreams.

June 20

Cleaning my study today, I discovered a fragment of verses I'd set aside to turn into a poem someday. This evening it seems complete:

> Oh the muscles
> after a season heaving
> only ideas!
>
> The ache breaks through
> the mind's weariness
> like the sun
> through winter clouds.